TRAGEDY TRANSFORMED

No case is as clear an example of the unity of the person, body, mind, and spirit, as that of biblical Job. Dr. Grose takes seriously Job's suffering in each area as he outlines the process of Job's recovery and gives examples from the lives of people today. In our society, where hurting people tend to choose between medical, psychological, and spiritual intervention, Dr. Grose affirms the value of all three.

HAROLD KOENIG, MD, MHSc, PROFESSOR OF PSYCHIATRY AND
BEHAVIORAL SCIENCES
ASSOCIATE PROFESSOR OF MEDICINE
DIRECTOR, CENTER FOR SPIRITUALITY, THEOLOGY, AND HEALTH
DUKE UNIVERSITY MEDICAL CENTER
DURHAM, NC

I am so grateful to Gordon for writing this book! He brings to life the story of Job and the stages of suffering that Job experiences. With real-life examples and clear explanations, he helps those of us who have experienced trauma gain a better understanding of the journey toward recovery. He also gives us practical tips for our journey.

SANDY WILSON, DMIN, RETIRED PROFESSOR WESTERN SEMINARY,
PORTLAND, OR,
CO-DIRECTOR OF TUFF STUFF MINISTRIES

"How do I recover from the tragedies of life?" "Where do I find hope?" "How do I renew my faith?" With sensitivity and skill, Dr. Gordon Grose answers these questions and more in *Tragedy Transformed*. If you, or someone you know, needs help to process and ultimately gain from pain, you'll find his experience and wisdom a comfort and a guide.

POPPY SMITH, MSFD
INSPIRATIONAL BIBLE TEACHER, MULTI-PUBLISHED AUTHOR,
SPIRITUAL COUNSELOR

Human suffering comes in many forms. Everyone suffers at times; some in small ways, some in large. Regardless of the form of suffering, a common human response is to question God. Some question God's character. Others question God's very existence. Dr. Gordon Grose has known suffering both through his work in counseling others and at a deep personal level. In his approach to Job he makes the questions about suffering confronted by Job and his friends a part of your story, my story and his story. The insights gleaned can help us to understand where God is and what God is doing when we experience pain and suffering.

RODGER K. BUFFORD, PHD, PROFESSOR OF PSYCHOLOGY
GRADUATE DEPARTMENT OF CLINICAL PSYCHOLOGY
GEORGE FOX UNIVERSITY, NEWBERG, OR
PSYCHOLOGIST, WESTERN PSYCHOLOGICAL AND COUNSELING
SERVICES, TIGARD, OR

Tragedy Transformed increases our perspective on how God works for His glory and for our good. As a theologian and as a counselor, Gordon Grose shows a rare gift for helping us come to grips with suffering. He also shows how God can use it to refine His children. A prime example of a godly response to nearly impossible extreme trials, Job comes through with the victory God provides. We all experience severe trials—how we approach them challenges us. This book offers sage advice with practical ways to help us face such tests. Along with squarely facing difficult issues, applying biblical principles leads toward finding solutions. *Tragedy Transformed* contains some of the best work I've read on mental health and spiritual wellness. This important information can help us make sense out of life, which frequently comes with unexplained challenges.

DR. GORDON BORROR, RETIRED PROFESSOR, SOUTHWESTERN
BAPTIST THEOLOGICAL SEMINARY,
FORT WORTH, TX, PASTOR AND CHURCH MUSICIAN

TRAGEDY
TRANSFORMED

TRAGEDY TRANSFORMED

How Job's Recovery Can Provide Hope for Yours

GORDON S. GROSE

Published in Partnership with:
BelieversPress
5585 Erindale Drive, Suite 200
Colorado Springs, CO 80918

Cover created by: Dugan Design

Interior created by: SP Design

Printed by: Bethany Press

Scripture references to Job are taken from Greenberg, Moshe, Jonas C.
Greenfield, and Nahum M. Sarna. *The Book of Job: A New Translation
According to the Traditional Hebrew Text with Introductions*. Philadelphia: The
Jewish Publication Society, 1980.

Scripture quotations marked NIV are taken from the *Holy Bible: New
International Version*®. NIV®. Copyright © 1973, 1978, 1984 by International
Bible Society. Used by permission of Zondervan Publishing House. All rights
reserved.

The "NIV" and "New International Version" trademarks are registered in the
United States Patent and Trademark Office by International Bible Society. Use
of either trademark requires permission of International Bible Society.

Scripture quotations marked NASB are taken from the New American Standard
Bible, © 1960, 1962, 1963, 1968, 1971, 1972, 1973, 1975, 1977, and 1995 the
Lockman Foundation, La Habra, Calif. Used by Permission.

Scripture quotations marked KJV are taken from *The Holy Bible, Authorized
King James* Version. Oxford: Oxford University Press, and London: Geoffrey
Cumberlege, 1611.

ISBNs:
Print: 978-0-578-16089-4
ePub: 978-0-578-16102-0
MOBI: 978-0-578-16103-7

LCCN: 2015905237

Printed in the United States of America

CONTENTS

DEDICATION

For Paul and Juli

FOREWORD

A LL TOO FREQUENTLY we are bombarded by the news
media with stories of suffering and pain from all over the
world. Added to this picture is the evidence of suffering
and pain that had crept into our own personal lives. In fact, so
prevalent has this topic been that it had already begun to take
pride of place all the way back in the Garden of Eden. There is
no question that this issue of the presence of evil, suffering, pain
and violence has troubled us time and time again. Why on earth
was it that God ever permitted evil to have any place in His creation? What purpose could such hurt and harm have in this creation of God? And even if its presence and final outcome were
decisively cared for in the Biblical story, that still leaves the issue
of the origin of suffering, pain and evil. Why did God ever allow
it to get started in the first place? That is the question that boggles
our minds. Why? Why? Why? Why did God permit evil to start?
So what is the origin of evil and suffering?

Yet, despite the presence and prominence of evil in the world,
we must in the same breath that we ask about the presence and
origin of evil ask our Lord about the presence of "goodness"
just as persistently. The presence of evil is just as puzzling as
the presence of God's evidences of his "goodness." As a matter
of fact, it has often happened precisely in our pain and suffering that God's goodness and existence becomes even more
apparent than it was for us prior to our meeting with pain and
suffering. A prominent example of such a combination of pain

along with the beauty of God's presence can be seen in Exodus 33:19. There in the scene of Aaron's Golden Calf debacle, God spoke to Moses on Mount Sinai and declared: "I will cause all my goodness to pass by in front of you and I will proclaim my name, the LORD, in your presence." Thus, the "goodness of God" was nothing less than all the qualities of the Living God. It included His character, His qualities, and all that He stood for in principle, power and authority.

No wonder, then, that a despairing prophet named Elijah, retreated to that same Mount Sinai, where he was divinely told to "Go out and stand on the mountain [Sinai] in the presence of the LORD, for the LORD is about to pass by" (1 Kings 19:11). Both narratives (the one about Moses and the one about Elijah) carry the verb "pass by," thereby urging us to view the two narratives together. As God refreshed Moses in the face of evil with a whole new vision of Himself and who He was in all of His fullness, so Elijah, deep in his despondency likewise needed a fresh view of who God was, even more so in the trying times such as these two men were wrestling with the problem of evil. Moreover, that is the same promise of "God's goodness" that is given to all of His own in that favorite Psalm, Psalm 23:6 – "Surely goodness and mercy shall follow me all the days of my life" (KJV). Likewise, the psalmist sang in Psalm 31:19, "How great is your goodness, which you have stored up for those who fear you, which you bestow in the sight of men on those who take refuge in you." The goodness of God is as much a problem as the problem of evil continued to be!

Therefore, even though it is most difficult in the midst of our pain to agree fully with what our Lord teaches us here, if we ever wish to gain a balanced view of the problem of suffering and pain, we must consider this suffering and pain in the context of the problem of the goodness of God. Since evil, suffering, pain and the violence of sin is such a huge part of our everyday experience in life, we have only one place to resort to and that is to the God of all grace and mercy. We go to His word to seek what insights he has given to us as we place His majesty, power and purpose over against our wounds.

That is why this book you hold in your hands has resorted to the Biblical book of Job to seek answers and perspective on this problem. Here was a case of one who was clearly an innocent sufferer. Who was more righteous than the man Job? Why, even God agreed with that evaluation, for that is why He suggested his name as the best candidate for such a title. Thus, while God is completely able to deliver Job, nevertheless He allows Satan to almost completely destroy this man to see if he will yield. Satan's wager was that every man or woman had their price. Given the right circumstances, everyone will curse God and abandon Him when it seems He has abandoned them and they no longer are seeing any evidence of His gifts in their lives. But the Devil loses his bet, for though Job will show he can still sin, yet he steadfastly refuses to curse God and forsake Him as his Lord and Savior.

This book, like the book of Job, will not give a set of complete answers to the problem of evil or to the problem of why God has sent so much of His goodness either; but it will point to many of the Biblical aids that will bring us to the point where the Lord can "Pass by" in front of us with a view of all his "goodness." May our Lord bless each reader to His honor and to His glory! And may what Gordon has pointed to in this book be of great help to all who now suffer and cry out to God, "How long, O LORD?" May God Himself pass by in front of you and show you all His goodness!!!!

Walter C. Kaiser, Jr.
President Emeritus
Gordon-Conwell Theological Seminary
Hamilton, MA

PART ONE

WHY TRANSFORMATION?

FROM DISASTER TO DESPAIR

CHAPTER 1

FACING THE UNAVOIDABLE

M Y WIFE ELAINE and I took one look at our son Paul's college room, then stared at each other. We saw: papers, books, clothes, bedding, dust, paperclips—and, as we got down on our knees to clean, dirt. Two days from his graduation, our son had nothing sorted, and nothing packed. We needed to box—and ship—everything in those two days.

Elaine and I felt proud to have our son attend our alma mater. Paul demonstrated academic achievement, musical gifts, and an outgoing personality. We knew he would go far.

"Stay close to the Lord." That was my last bit of counsel four years earlier in our last moments together. I said my piece, then I left him to introduce himself to new classmates. Now here we were knee-deep in the multiplied stuff he accumulated in those four years.

Paul wasn't immune to the concern that showed on our faces. He defended himself, "But, Dad and Mom, I had to help Juli." He was right, he did.

Six weeks earlier Paul's fiancée, Juli, came down with infectious mononucleosis. Too weak to attend classes, she needed daily tutoring. In addition to completing his studies, Paul stepped in to help Juli keep up her classwork so she could graduate.

But it wasn't just graduation that weighed heavily. The couple's wedding was looming closer even than graduation. Juli's dad, the Rev. Jim Andrews and I were going to conduct the ceremony together. Some friends the couple wanted to participate—bridesmaids, groomsmen, and performers in a string quartet—were children of missionary parents. The day after graduation, they would depart for destinations around the world. The only day to have everyone together was the day *before* graduation.

Elaine and I, anticipating the pleasure of Paul's wedding and graduation, felt angry that he'd left the cleaning of his room for us. But we weren't the only ones to face disappointment. Because of the need to clean Juli's room, her mother Olsie didn't even make it to their graduation. That was the initial impact of Juli's illness on Paul and all of us parents. That impact didn't lessen in the years that followed.

THE COST OF TRAGEDY

Tragedy like this penetrates our comfortable routine with a crisis impossible to avoid. It costs us time, attention, and sometimes money. I don't know the tragedy you've encountered, but it's probably forced you to face something you'd rather have avoided: disaster, incurable illness, or significant loss. You may have done nothing to contribute to your heartache, but you nevertheless face the overwhelming task of getting through the next day, hour, minute—if only you knew how.

I wish you didn't need this book, but I've written it because I know you do. I hope our family's story will help you think about your story, when your world turns upside down.

You may be looking for easy answers, but instead I hope to help you explore the hard questions.

After a tragedy, it's easy to get stuck. We can end up traumatized, depressed, or bitter—or all three. We can withdraw from important relationships. We can blame God and withdraw from Him as well. Whatever your circumstances and wherever you are in your recovery from tragedy, I want to use our family's experience, the stories of other people, and Job's story from God's Word to help you through.

At Paul's graduation my world began to turn upside down; tragedy snuck up on me. After six months, Paul also developed mononucleosis. Mono for each led to myalgic encephalomyelitis, also known as chronic fatigue syndrome.[1] Juli later developed multiple chemical sensitivities and experienced *vasculitis*, a painful inflammation of her blood vessels upon chemical exposure. For years, I resisted facing it, but my son and daughter-in-law's medical condition forced me to change my thinking, my habits, and my relationship with God. We never know when we will confront an overwhelming, inescapable demand to deal with tragedy.

Although the crises come less often these days, Elaine and I still never know when our son will need us to pick up a prescription or, unable to leave Juli, ask me to buy plumbing supplies on a Sunday morning because he accidentally broke their water pipes.

JOB: MY FAVORITE BIBLE BOOK

As we hunt for ways to grapple with personal tragedies, many people turn to the most famous story of personal tragedy we know—Job. "Job is my favorite book of the Bible," people tell me. "The things that happened to him..." they say, their voice trailing off. Job's story helps them put their problems into perspective; in light of Job's tragedies, theirs seem minuscule.

But reading Job's story for consolation, insight, or perspective

creates difficulties. Like most of us, I tune in better to the prose
of the story than to the poetic dialogue. As a result, when I read
the book, I grasp the storyline at the beginning (the first two
chapters) and at the end (the last chapter), but I find the disputes
between Job and his friends tedious. I bog down in their well-
meaning, but hurtful counsel, even when I read some elements
of truth in what they say. I also find the long speeches toward
the end wearing. *What's the point?*

I've studied these sections again and again, though. And in
them I see huge benefits. I write, therefore, to help us benefit from
the large central section, the part we tend to skip. After careful
study, that's where I found the greatest treasure to deal with my
tragedy. In the poetry of the dialogues with his wisdom colleagues,
Job's recovery comes to light. When I face the worst life brings,
teasing out the life-lessons from Job's inner experience through the
middle of his story gives me hope. If Job gets better, maybe I can,
too. If you need hope to recover from your tragedy, maybe Job's
story can also provide that hope for you.

THE BIG QUESTION

When we're going through tragedy, one important question
arises: Where is God? Easy answers, like He's the sun above the
clouds, trivialize our hurt; complex answers, like God's omnipotence (He does what He wants), frustrate us; yet receiving no
answer at all may seem to confirm our worst suspicions—God
has forgotten us, abandoned us to Fate. If you've questioned
God's presence in tragedy, however, you'll find in Job's story at
least the kernel of an answer. Job not only feels abandoned, but
with great eloquence, he tells God about it. And, in a surprise,
God responds, though not in the way Job expects.

Whatever tragedy we've experienced, Job's story can encourage
us, because through it we become aware of God's very real

presence. But it also warns us that the Sovereign Lord is not subject to our demands for answers.

The answer Job receives rocks him every bit as much as his tragedies.

Job's story, then, is our story. Along with observing his response to tragedy, we will see people today in tragedies similar to his. We'll learn about their faith amid horrible life circumstances. Through no fault of our own at any point tragedy can disrupt our lives, cause untold grief, and, if we survive, change us forever.

When unusual physical illnesses immobilized Paul and Juli, tragedy hit our whole extended family. When two state police officers with unwelcome news rang her doorbell, tragedy ambushed Melissa. Tragedy struck Andrea and her family when Hurricane Katrina's waters flooded their city, church building, and home.

In the pages that follow, these modern-day fellow sufferers let us in on their real and poignant struggles as they faced strange physical illness, a natural disaster, a serious mental disorder, and insurmountable grief. They'll show us how they've come to live a new normal—and how, even as victims of tragedy, they can and have recovered. Job's story and theirs can provide you the hope you need for your recovery. Because they recovered, you can too.

How Do I
LEARN TO FACE THE UNAVOIDABLE?

1. In the light of people mentioned in chapter 1, reflect on your friends and family who have faced tragedy. How common, for example, is tragedy in their lives? How serious? How did they cope? How involved were you in their recovery?

2. In addition to Job, identify other Bible characters who experienced dramatic losses, physical suffering, and/or mental anguish.

3. Ask others close to you who experienced sadness or tragedy what life lessons they learned through their experience.

4. Note at least three tragedies from your daily newspaper or Internet home page.

CHAPTER 2

TRAGEDY TRANSFORMED THROUGH OBSERVING JOB'S RECOVERY

URRICANE KATRINA IS among the worst natural disasters in U.S. history. In late August 2005, satellite images filled TV screens nationwide with the expected trajectory of a massive, growing, and dangerous Category Three hurricane. Again and again, forecasters charted the course of this storm destined to hit a key piece of real estate—below sea level. Nearby, next to Lake Ponchartrain in a New Orleans suburb, Mike and Andrea lived with their seven children.

I survived Hurricane Betsy and Camille, Mike thought. *I'll ride out this one, too.*

"I don't feel good about this," Andrea told him. "But I'm determined to stick with you."

A church friend called Mike just then. "I know this is

unusual, but we've cancelled Sunday services." After ashen-faced Mike hung up, the word *Go!* echoed through his head.

Andrea was the first to come up with a plan. "Let's all go to Memphis." Her parents lived there. So Mike and Andrea, their seven children, and Andrea's wheelchair-bound mother who had been visiting scrambled into their van, only to inch along, bumper-to-bumper, on a jammed highway. With red brake lights as far as the eye could see, they had no idea the usual six-and-a-half-hour drive would take them more than eleven.

"As we drove, I recalled how, the previous Sunday, our church had sung, 'Blessed Be Your Name,'" Andrea said. The lyrics to that song, incidentally quote a post-disaster Job praising God despite it all. "*What if that happened to you?* I wondered at the time." Andrea remembers telling God, *Take anything. Just don't take my family.*

When they arrived in Memphis, relatives and local church people took them in. Yet Andrea admits to ambivalence. "Even though we were safe, my internal battle with God raged." Andrea's most pressing and practical question was, *How are we going to make ends meet?*

RECOVERY AND TRANSFORMATION

Before we return to Andrea and Mike's story of recovery and transformation, let's open with a few principles you may or may not buy into at this stage. Trust me, though, I've experienced the stages of tragedy and grief—and these principles do prove to be true over time.

The first principle is that tragedies such as the destruction of property, life-threatening illness, financial failure, and the sudden death of a loved one can create deep sadness, even despair. Although intense grief is normal in tragedy, when our emotions overwhelm us, our thinking, feeling, and decision-making abilities will suffer. The daunting tasks of recovery tax the strongest among us. Recovery, then, will not be an easy or an automatic task.

The next principle is this: With help we can begin to function as our normal selves once again. We may not see it at the moment of our deepest grief, but a new normal will come in time. Belief in the involvement of a personal God who cares about us also can help us recover. In recovery, as much as possible, we attempt to restore ourselves to where we were before our loss. At the same time, beyond our immediate needs for recovery, we may discover ways our tragedy has transformed us—changed us for the better.

That transformation may be the best-case outcome of our facing tragedy head-on. There's a principle in nature that transformation can lead to greater usefulness. Nature transformed a hazelnut a squirrel buried in my backyard into a small plant. That plant possessed potential to develop into an adult tree, with further potential to transform into reproducing hazelnuts. Without the burial, none of that potential, none of that transformation would have come.

How can tragedy transform us into something better? One way is that it may transform our perspective on life—and death. Through it we may acquire greater wisdom. Our relationship with God also can deepen. All of these changes can transform us to make us more useful to ourselves, to others, and perhaps to God.

Yet, we may not be able to gain that kind of positive perspective in the moment. Often tragedy blindsides us—as it likely has done to you. Like Mike and Andrea, have you endured overwhelming natural disaster? As you think about a loved one or friend you miss, do tears well? Has an unexpected diagnosis scared you? Or has long-term joblessness triggered depression? Do you despair for the point of your life? Or of life itself? Given sufficient emotional pain, you may indeed feel despair, which I'd define as the loss of hope. While others go on with their lives, despair makes you feel stuck.

Seeking Hope in Despair

If anyone should feel entitled to fall into despair and remain there for life, it is Job. Yet God brings him *through* tragedy and into a new life. Job witnessed the destruction of his businesses, as you may have. He heard of his children's home flattened. Your home may also have been ruined. He learned of the murder of his employees. Your family may also have been a victim of violence. He loses all his children. You may have lost one or more of yours.

From his loss of businesses, employees, and children, to scraping his boils in isolation on an ash heap, Job's tragedies accumulate. "Curse God and die!" his wife commands him.

As the unfairness of his suffering torments him, he calls to God in despair, "Your hands shaped and fashioned me, then destroyed every part of me."

What do we learn from his story? We find an example of someone who suffers through no fault of his own. From him we learn our vulnerability to tragedy. We watch him descend into despair, protest against injustice, and seek out God in an attempt to plead his case. We observe his subtle shift from helpless victim of circumstances to a take-charge attitude about his life. We hear his friends' futile attempts to console him with pat answers, yet also notice the good they bring. We see how Job recovers from trauma, despair, and grief. Then, meeting God, he's transformed. The entire process changes how we understand Job. No longer simply a victim of tragedy, he now provides a model of hope that we, too, can recover as he did.

But transformation from tragedy doesn't occur quickly—or easily. We don't "just get over it." Andrea and Mike didn't. Job didn't. We won't either. It may involve a long, sometimes painful process of recovery. But transformation does happen.

With Job as our prime example, let's explore the transformation of tragedy. We will learn how to regain hope, recover mental and physical wholeness, and find a deeper relationship with God.

How Long Will This Take?

Like the healing of our body, recovery, healing, and transformation after tragedy involve taking many small steps in succession. In this case, we base each act or decision on where we find hope. Transformation, therefore, implies the passage of time—time needed for change.

You may expect a quick fix. Some demand it. They seek a counselor or doctor who agrees to provide a prescription, or they use alcohol or other chemicals to quiet their pain. Like a jilted lover on the rebound, Job pursues a quick fix—an immediate confrontation with God to clear his good name. But instead he learns recovery takes time. Transformation may take even longer.

Recovery may not only take time to accomplish, but it may also take time to begin. Ann wore a black dress, her eyes red. As my wife and I waited at the end of the long receiving line after her husband's memorial service at church, my heart ached for everything she was going through. After the others left, we hugged her.

"We're so sorry," I said. "We'll miss Jim so much. Tell us how you're doing."

"I'm okay," she said, her face flushed. "But it's going to be hard raising the kids." For the next several minutes, we talked about her children, her needs, and her husband.

Jim's serious ailment had forced the couple to retire from a productive ministry in South America and return home. Thanks to a complicated operation, Jim successfully battled the disease for years. Then because of infection, he lost the war. After years of hospitalizations, toxic medication, and constant worry, how could he die of a simple infection? He and Ann thought they'd seen the worst of it. Now, how could she, a young mother, cope with three youngsters alone?

"I'm writing a book on transforming tragedy," I told her.

"I'd like to read that," she replied, but then paused. "...at some point." Her pause let me know, "I'm not ready." You may not be ready, either.

Why does it take so long to begin? For one thing, recovery stirs emotional pain. Each step—fraught with hurtful memories, difficult emotions, and intensified grief—takes time to face and relive.

A woman who attended one of my presentations on overcoming grief told the group about her husband's death two years earlier. "He was tall. When I have to get something off the top shelf, that's when I miss him." Her choked voice trailed off. Every time she needed something up high, the memory of her tall husband triggered the pain of her loss.

There's another reason transformation after tragedy takes time: it involves a lot of change. You may not feel ready for change; you may resist or deny it. Grief can be a slow process. Adjusting to a new reality and accepting your changed circumstances can take even longer to face.

WHAT TRANSFORMATION IS NOT

In describing transformation, I do not offer a series of orderly levels, stages, or fixes. Transformation involves progress and backtracking; it requires patience. You will *resolve* an issue only to find it reappear and require reworking again—and again. Elizabeth Kübler-Ross, well known for her "five stages of grief," knew people didn't grieve in neat emotional stages. In a 1981 Santa Barbara lecture, I heard her describe her stages as artificial constructs to organize her 1969 book, *On Death and Dying*. And we thought we had found the formula.

I have found no neat formula in Job or in life. Some griefs

we may never fully resolve, but I hope you will find strength to move on. Job's story provides vital principles of transformation to help us progress through the most painful life experiences.

You may find relief, for example, when Job voices your secret thoughts about God's abandonment. Or his words could trigger your strong feelings of abandonment. You may find hope from the interviews with people who've experienced massive disaster. Or their strong faith could put you off. You may identify with the many emotions Job and others report. Or the information on trauma, abuse, and neglect could trigger painful memories.

No matter, you can find hope in transformation. When heat transforms into steam, the water remains although it changes form. When God transforms your tragedy, you remain the same, yet with a changed perspective on loss, life, and God. Job had to go through a long period of recovery to appreciate the answers he received and be transformed by them.

I encourage you, though, to start at the beginning. If you skip to the end of the story, you could short-circuit your transformation.

TRANSFORMATION RAISES QUESTIONS

As with many valuable life lessons, we begin with real, heart-felt questions: *How* do we recover from disaster, live with debilitating illness, and grieve our losses? *Where* do we find hope? Beyond recovery, *how* do we renew our faith?

Because Scripture presents Job's story in complicated literary forms of rounds of dialogues and long monologues, we may miss his progress.

As I traced his response to tragedy, after an initial period of hopelessness, I noticed him getting better. But *how*? How does Job go from wanting to die in chapter 3 to meeting God in chapter 38? I dug deep in my studies of the book to find the answer. If we understand how Job heals, maybe his story can help us heal. In the same way, when we look back on earlier times in life and compare them with our present, our own progress may surprise us.

Throughout Job's recovery, we also may ask, What emotions does he show that are similar to mine? What helped him deal with those emotions? One factor stands out: even in his most despairing times, Job pursued God.

You may reject the idea of a Supreme Being as being unscientific. Perhaps your ethical beliefs make the idea of God unnecessary. You may feel so angry with Him for the way He allowed people to mistreat you, that you refuse to acknowledge Him. Or maybe you just don't know whether there is a God. The ease with which I seem to assume the reality of God and His intervention in people's lives may, perhaps, tempt you to stop reading.

I make no apologies for the God described in the Book of Job or in the stories of people I recount. Job's story assumes a personal God who acts, speaks, and heals the brokenhearted. But I hope you find much common ground in Job's tragedies, which are universal, and in his transformation, which can offer you hope.

Job's story raises the issue of God's silence during suffering. God even seems absent at times, yet He speaks at the most unexpected moment. Why doesn't He speak sooner? Do you also wish God would speak sooner to you? Now? Maybe, as with Job, you need to give Him a piece of your mind, to pour out your grief, or to demand to know why you're facing this tragedy. Or maybe you just need the comfort of His presence.

Job's friends raise still other issues. This book considers only the first of three "rounds" of his discussions with his friends, but enough to learn how they understand his trials (chapters 4-14). As their dialogue continues, the friends' opinions of Job only intensify. Our friends and loved ones may be every bit as imperfect as Job's friends. They may not always know the right thing to do or say, but they can still help—a lot. Others want to help—friends, loved ones, doctors, pastors, and counselors. God, too, may be a lot closer than we feel.

What *do* you feel? What decisions can you make, which in the end will help you feel better? How can you enable yourself, others, and God to make the changes necessary for your health, sanity, and a deeper relationship with Him? When you look back, even now, what positive changes do you see?

THE TRANSFORMATION OF JOB'S TRAGEDY

We'll follow Job's transformation by dividing his story into three phases: from disaster to despair, from despair to recovery, and from recovery to transformation. I have organized this book into the same parts:

- Part One: Why Transformation? *(From disaster to despair)*: Here we explore the reasons for despair—from Job's life and from some of our contemporaries.

- Part Two: Recovery—Steps toward Transformation. *(From despair to recovery)*: As Job expresses anger with God, three friends, even in disagreement, provide him with critical social support. They also teach us valuable lessons on how to support others through their tragedies.

- Part Three: A Model of Transformation. *(From recovery to transformation)*: Another friend helps Job listen—not always easy for him or for us. With better listening, offering common ground, and a renewed focus on God, Job's fourth friend prepares him for what comes next. After preparation through listening—and confrontation—in a surprise, Job meets God. As God reveals Himself, He also reveals His transforming perspective on Job's tragedy. We'll learn with Job what God might say to us.

I believe through these three sections you'll see how no tragedy is too great that we can't recover and grow closer to God. If you are ready, let's begin the journey in earnest.

How Do I
Live with Questions?

1. Write down at least three questions you have about tragedy.

2. Identify to whom you would like to address those questions—friends, family, your pastor, a godly friend, the author, God, etc.?

3. Begin to collect the questions you have on tragedy in a notebook or journal.

4. What question(s) would you like to ask Job?

5. Find a friend or group with whom to share your questions—without expecting answers, but just to hear you share your questions. Invite them to share theirs with you.

CHAPTER 3

WHEN MY WORLD TURNS UPSIDE DOWN

BECAUSE TRAGEDY SADDENS us, we often avoid thinking about it. A glance at our daily headlines reveals numerous tragedies, whose details we may avoid. We can deal with only so much. When we hear of misfortune, we switch channels, click on another link, or change the subject. But reverses don't only happen to others; they also happen to us. However hard we strive to avoid misfortune, at times even our best efforts fail: our world turns upside down.

No one welcomes tragedy, but to acknowledge unexpected reverses can protect us from overconfidence. Life *is* fragile: accidents, illness, suicide, war, deaths, and injuries intrude.

To understand our vulnerability to natural disaster, we'll look more closely at Mike and Andrea's encounter with Katrina.

FROM UNREAL TO HOPELESS

Memphis news reports detailed the loss of power to thousands, with no way to communicate with people in New Orleans because of downed phone lines. Stories of flooding, looting, gunfire, disease, and evacuations filled the airwaves. Katrina's residual effects were catastrophic.

This is not really happening. That was Andrea's first thought. *We're going to get back and it's not going to be that bad.* After a couple of months safe in Memphis, however, Andrea felt differently.

"I felt depressed from not knowing what happened to our home, community, jobs, or church. Satan does that to you. I felt hopeless. I didn't have accurate information to offset all the bad news in the media."

With so many deaths, homes destroyed, citizens displaced, and sheer amount of misery, Hurricane Katrina created an incomprehensible national tragedy. "City Spirals into Chaos" read the headline of my daily newspaper four days after Katrina struck New Orleans. "Medical helicopters and law officers come under fire. Survivors battle for seats on the buses that would carry them away from the nightmare. The tired, hungry and desperate seethe, saying they have been forsaken."[1] People everywhere despaired.

To salvage what they could, Mike and their oldest daughter returned home two weeks later. "I was in shock at what I saw," Mike said. Even before reaching their home, they had observed a 200-foot swath with no trees.

"That was a tornado," Mike said. As they exited the interstate highway, the storm had left seemingly endless piles of debris on both sides of the street: leaves and tree limbs. A few days later, when they visited their church, they saw the south side of town, where a nearby lake had overflowed, piling whole neighborhoods with tree debris, trash, and garbage twelve to fifteen feet high.

Passing by homes in their neighborhood, they observed a water line twelve to eighteen inches above ground level. To reach their front door, they brushed aside the branches of their front yard tree. The giant tree had split lengthwise, with one half still standing, the other half resting in their crushed roof. Inside, everything looked clean, although in the semi-darkness they spotted a two-foot high green watermark on the walls.

They gagged. Their particle masks couldn't keep out the odor, nor prevent their salivary glands from secreting the taste of death. Their shoes squished as they traced the awful stench to the refrigerator, where—without power—their meat had rotted. When Andrea and the rest of the family returned two months later, their rented home remained unlivable, green with mold. It had not yet been gutted.

"I don't want you staying in your house," a kind friend said, as she welcomed the family into her home.

After two months of living with this friend, though, they felt in need of their own place. Without housekeeping, Andrea also had too much time on her hands. Those factors combined to trigger another bout of depression. "Again I felt hopeless—not knowing what was going to happen."

In December, Mike, Andrea and their family moved back to their rental house. To avoid the mold, the children slept in the center of the room on bunk beds—away from the walls.

Because Mike and Andrea's mattress, though not the box spring, had stayed dry, they also slept in their bedroom. When they received a trailer from the Federal Emergency Management Agency (FEMA) on the property, the family used it to cook and to sleep. The children played in the trailer and used the path inside their home, cleared for real estate agents, to ride bikes and roller skate.

Do you smile at this last statement? In the middle of this huge dislocation, Mike and Andrea's children roller-skated on a path through their ruined house. Your tragedy may also present ironic if not humorous sidelights: a small but sentimental item rescued from a house fire, or a bookmark placed at a key passage before the sudden death of a loved one. The bleakness of your tragedy may be temporarily relieved by some seemingly insignificant event as it provides a glimmer of meaning. Unrelieved tragedy burdens us too much.

I Can't Go on Like This

Squeezed between her need to help her students displaced by Hurricane Katrina, her need to care for her children, living in a ruined house, and not knowing where cleanup workers stored her belongings, again Andrea approached despair. "Contractors would fix something, but it would be weeks before you'd see them again."

"God, I just can't go on living like this." Andrea collapsed near the door of her trailer one day.

"*That's what I'm here for,* God seemed to say. *You don't need to do everything on your own. I'm here. I'm going to help you.*" She recalls that at last a peace settled on her.

"That was my problem. I was trying to do it all on my own; I wasn't trusting God."

"Then, on May 1, we got an eviction notice for June 1," Andrea said. The owners couldn't fix or sell their home. Mike and Andrea had to vacate the trailer, too. But with no place to go. Because rent in the area had quadrupled, they struggled to find an affordable house.

To Mike and Andrea's relief, one woman offered for them to stay in a FEMA trailer on her property. After they settled in, however, their hostess surprised them. "I've been diagnosed with breast cancer," she said. "I hate to do this, but I really need this time with my family." Once again they had to move.

Andrea and her family lived in another FEMA trailer a few days when they learned of an available rental. Even though the landlord charged three times their previous month's rent, they moved in, relieved, "able to breathe." They grew closer as a family. "From August to August," Andrea recounted, "we moved six times."

Imagine yourself a homemaker, with seven children, a husband, and a job, moving again and again. How would you cope? Multiply Mike and Andrea's experience many thousands of times for the lives of other Katrina victims.

FEAR, DOUBT, UNANSWERED PRAYER

Even Mike, who had lived through other hurricanes, hadn't expected this to be as devastating. Rolling back the clock, he recalls that because of his work as a hearing specialist, he returned to the area six times to service hearing aids, before his family joined him there. During those visits, he stayed with church families. "The damage was unimaginable. I had lived through two major hurricanes, but they weren't as destructive."

Yet, he worried. "I was scared we were going to be homeless or have to live with someone else a long time. I hate imposing. This was their family, and we're right in the middle of them. I didn't know what to do."

That first year Mike prayed all the time, but without a positive answer. *What's going to happen? Aren't You going to answer my prayer? What have I done so bad You're not going to help?* "That's the way I was raised. It's all by works, by reward.

"God turned his back on me, and I feel bad because my family has to take the consequences."

In addition to fear, doubt, and despair, he felt guilty that his family had to suffer for what he saw as his failure.

UNDERSTANDABLE RESPONSES

Our hearts go out to people like Mike and Andrea and their children—forced from a secure family life in a safe home. We wonder what we would do in similar circumstances. How would we hold up? Would we also feel depressed? Would we also question God? Would we also blame ourselves?

Perhaps you've not been through a hurricane, but maybe you know what it's like to survive a blizzard, drought, tornado, wild-fire, flood, or heat wave. During one recent year, each of those natural disasters caused over $1 billion in damages in the U.S., with much loss of human life.[2] You never thought you would see the day the forces of nature would wreak so much havoc. Now you know how vulnerable you are—we all are.

Such disasters as Mike and Andrea experienced have been occur-ring since the beginning of mankind. In the Bible, for example, from a life of material success, we learn of Job's quick succession of violent losses. Despite his exceptional efforts, he also experiences misfortune. As he discovers, we cannot always control events.

A SERENE LIFE

There was a man in the land of Uz named Job. That man was blameless and upright: he feared God and shunned evil...His possessions were seven thousand sheep, three thou-sand camels, five hundred yoke of oxen and five hundred she-asses, and a very large household. That man was wealthier than anyone in the East (Job 1:1-3).[3]

A model of righteous character, Job also enjoys great material blessings. Seven thousand sheep reveal his business prowess. Three thousand camels point to his mastery of transport. Five hundred yoke of oxen and five hundred donkeys demonstrate his domi-nance in agriculture.[4] Job's livestock requires careful tending by a huge staff. His barns dot the hillside. Large tracts of cultivated land and pastures stretch to the horizon. We hear the bleating, snorting, and hee-hawing.

"Wealthier than anyone in the East," Job enjoys everything of importance in his time and society—vast possessions, ideal family, ethical character, and genuine faith. Although busy with staff overseeing huge agricultural, transportation, and meat-producing enterprises, he pays close attention to one matter in particular.

When a round of feast days was over, Job would send word to [his children] to sanctify themselves, and, rising early in the morning, he would make burnt offerings for each of them; for Job thought, "Perhaps my children have sinned and blasphemed God in their thoughts." This is what Job always used to do (Job 1:5).

When life goes well, what do we think about? To a CEO, doesn't the thought on occasion surface: what could go wrong? If it doesn't, it should. Executive responsibilities include risk assessment. Would he or she not take preemptive action to forestall misfortune—hire a new manager, fire an unproductive employee, or call a staff trouble-shooting meeting? If we've struggled with such thoughts, we can appreciate that one other detail about Job.

"Knock on wood," we say, as we rap our knuckles to maintain good fortune. With a touch of magical thinking, we expect our actions can affect our wellbeing. At times, of course, they do—but not always. Fearing the worst, we may even intensify our efforts, as Job does.

Job's business success or secure family life, however, cannot quash a persistent, nagging thought: in secret, had his children blasphemed God? He had toiled years to build wealth, but his children had it given them. His brow furrows. *Spiritually, have they drifted? Do they see God blocking their fun? Or worse, as their enemy? Had they secretly cursed...?*

Wary, Job needs reassurance. To deal with his fear, as patriarch Job "always" atones for his children's possible spiritual defection, even an impulsive or stray thought to curse God. Believing parents know what it's like to feel a spiritual burden for their children. Will they develop their own personal relationship with God? Will they reject the faith in which they've been raised?

Job's sacrifices strike us as unusual. Perhaps he simply performed his patriarchal responsibilities, as his intercession for his friends in chapter 42 shows.[5] Perhaps he reflects the normal concern of godly parents for the spiritual welfare of their children. Or do we understand something more? If he isn't unusual here, why mention it? This detail concludes the introduction to Job, which begins with the report of his righteousness. His repeated sacrifices, then, epitomize that righteousness. They also, he believes, enable him to maintain some control. Much like Mike, Job assumes misfortune results from personal transgression. Events on one particular day, however, shatter his serene existence. They also challenge his assumption about tragedy.

SERENITY DESTROYED

One day, as his sons and daughters were eating and drinking wine in the house of their eldest brother, a messenger came to Job and said, "The oxen were plowing and the asses were grazing alongside them when Sabeans attacked them and carried them off, and put the boys to the sword; I alone have escaped to tell you" (Job 1:13–15).

His eldest son's party brings together Job's children. At the same time, on a routine day at the farm, his servants transport equipment and seed by donkey. As the animals graze, exhausted, oxen take over to plow. Job lives at peace. Against this serene background, chaos, pillage, and death intrude. Sabeans, members of a caravan based miles south, drive off his livestock and murder his employees. Job suffers the total loss of his agricultural business. Only one fortunate servant escapes to report; Job's life changes forever.

That's the nature of tragedy. The crash of a car, a heart attack, the birth of a child with a handicap, all of those events—and countless others—change our lives forever. But that's still not the end of Job's troubles. His losses accumulate.

This one was still speaking when another came and said, "God's fire fell from heaven, took hold of the sheep and the boys, and burned them up; I alone have escaped to tell you" (Job 1:16).

In the middle of a sole survivor's report of a deadly enemy attack, another servant interrupts to report a natural disaster that wipes out Job's flocks and shepherds. The disastrous nature of the phenomenon far exceeds normal lightning storms coming east from the Mediterranean.[6] When it falls, it takes hold to burn up Job's flocks and shepherds. Another lone survivor escapes.

Job's losses accelerate. We assume that one disaster suffices for us to learn whatever life has to teach. But we enjoy no guarantee.

This one was still speaking when another came and said, "A Chaldean formation of three columns made a raid on the camels and carried them off and put the boys to the sword; I alone have escaped to tell you" (Job 1:17).

By their deployment of three raiding parties, the Chaldeans demonstrate thorough military planning.[7] They destroy Job's investments in trade through transportation. When we read of all Job's tragedies, we wonder how he can go on. Multiple setbacks, as with Mike and Andrea, can make living seem impossible. Today, middle-aged adults sometimes must face the health crises of their parents at the same time their children deal with addiction. Or the loss of a job can cascade to loss of healthcare, foreclosure, and homelessness. When crises come in rapid succession, how can we cope?

This one was still speaking when another came and said, "Your sons and daughters were eating and drinking in the house of their eldest brother when suddenly a mighty wind came from the wilderness. It struck the four corners of the house so that it collapsed upon the young people and they died; I alone have escaped to tell you" (Job 1:18–19).

Repetition further overwhelms Job. The hot east wind from the desert destroys what Job counts most important: his children. Before the storm, their joyous eating and drinking provide a paradigm of unexpected disaster. This lone surviving servant describes a tornado. From businesses to employees to beloved children, he loses more than we can imagine.

With no apparent reason why Job should suffer such tragedy, his experience strikes us as ironic. "The man was blameless and upright; he feared God and shunned evil" (1:1). His righteousness was impeccable. His sense of responsibility for his family, moreover, also exceeded expectations. If Job's experience is any guide, we cannot count on our own moral rectitude or on our ability to provide for others to prevent disaster. We have to admit we're vulnerable.

Along with natural disasters, the death of Job's children illustrates another common form of tragedy, untimely death. Sometimes one type gives rise to the other. In the months after Katrina, for example, the suicide rate in New Orleans doubled.[8] That's a factor we'll add to the mix in the next chapter.

How Do I
Live With My Upside Down World?

1. When you hear of others' misfortune, instead of changing the channel or subject, determine to learn more. Find out how the accident, illness, or death occurred. Learn about the people involved and their response.

2. Make a risk-assessment inventory of your life. Identify the ways your life is most fragile (e.g., health, relationships, home on a flood plain, etc.).

3. Create a plan to strengthen your areas of vulnerability. Think about those areas you can't control. Can you identify them? Reflect on what you can and can't control. Practice effecting change in those areas you can.

CHAPTER 4

WANTING TO DIE, CHOOSING NOT TO

SOMETIMES TRAGEDY HITS so hard we want to give up. *I've lost everything,* we think. *What's the use?* Even if we scream bloody murder, what good would that do? So we look for a way out. Because sharing our thoughts would scare the daylights out of our family, we don't. Several years ago, Peter faced that very crisis.

WANTING TO DIE

Peter's poem, *Who Owns My Life?* expresses his feelings about his life. It begins:

> Pain and anguish tear at my heart, the only relief
> from this world to part.
> Knife at wrist, mind's relief—it does send the
> thought of pain soon to an end.

How did Peter arrive at such despair? Peter had dreamed he and his wife would teach together in a Christian ministry. But after his marriage ended, so did that dream. Another factor: "I never resolved my divorce," he said. One reason for that failure—the church. "At that time," he said, "churches didn't know what to do with divorced people. I felt church people abandoned me. I determined never to be part of a church again." As a result, he turned to drinking, partying, and having a good time.

But after his second marriage also ended, "divorce devastated me," Peter said. "From childhood, my father taught me responsibility for myself and for my family. As a result, I worked hard to provide for and to protect my family." He worked decades for a company with a recognizable brand name. He looked forward to a comfortable retirement. But after his second divorce, "I thought I would have to work the rest of my life," he said. "I paid alimony. I no longer dreamed of retirement." That divorce required division of his property. Forced to give up a home in suburbs, their vacation home on a lake, two motorcycles, and two luxury cars, Peter felt little hope. "The vacation home," he said, "meant a place of retreat not only for my family, but also for important friends. With my divorce, I lost that. I lost friends, even one couple who had been in our wedding." But after the divorce, he also feared losing another important family relationship.

As movers removed his wife's belongings, Peter says, "I made a decision to keep the hose to a sump pump just in case." It fitted the tailpipe and extended long enough to reach into a car window. Prepared, Peter's losses culminated in one particular night of despair. "Suicide became a real possibility," he says "I planned a dress rehearsal to see what suicide would be like—if I could do it. I focused on ending all the pain. I saw death as a welcome relief."

It sounds trite to say that we're not the only one to face such a momentous, fearful, and life-threatening decision. Knowing others have faced similar struggles, however, and have come out the other side, can encourage us to hang on just a little longer. Our delay provides opportunity for longer-term help—and our survival.

Faith didn't protect several major Bible figures from despair, either, yet they survived temporary feelings of hopelessness to serve God and others. Although Elijah asks the Lord to take his life, and Jonah and Jeremiah ask to die, Job expresses the most intense, prolonged despair. His words in chapter 3 reveal someone who, like Peter, lost all hope. After the reports of devastation, Job remained steadfast in God's defense—at first. "Shall we accept good from God and not evil?" he asked his wife in chapter 2.

Stunned, unable to respond on an emotional level, initially Job clings to what he knows: he trusts God.

Perhaps some painful experience has you stunned. You don't know what to say, what to think, or how to feel, let alone what to do. So you hold on to what you already know. You stick with what you already believe. That helps hold you together—for now. Eventually, however, in a delayed response, as you begin to feel your distress more, like Job, an inner volcano rumbles. Soon, you may be unable to hold back. Like Mike and Andrea, we are all vulnerable to tragedy—and, like Andrea, Peter and Job, to despair.

With the aid of friends, time, and silence Job begins to feel his tragedies. In chapter 3, he erupts with a blast of red-hot verbal magma, the lava of despair. He speaks for many who've lost hope. What he says doesn't sound pretty—or spiritual. He may speak for you.

WORDS BITTER BUT HONEST

Afterward, Job began to speak and cursed the day of his birth. Job spoke up and said, "Perish the day on which I was born, and the night it was announced, 'A male had been conceived!'" (Job 3:1-3).

Desperate people say outlandish things. When Job finally speaks, he delivers a raging curse on the day of his birth. "May that day be darkness," he says of his birth. "May that night be barren," he says of his conception. Fifteen times Job uses the words translated as "may" or "let" to curse aspects of his life of suffering. Although he resists Satan's earlier prediction that, should he lose everything he would curse God,[1] Job comes close—very close. His birthday represents a safe target; he still determines not to curse God. With multiple curses he cries for the peace of the grave. In verse 10, he even curses the morning stars of his birthday, wishing they had remained dark because the dawn "did not block my mother's womb and hide trouble from my eyes." By trouble Job means "misery."[2]

In ancient Hebrew culture, success signified God's blessing and failure represented God's curse. Likewise, when a Hebrew with social standing such as Job utters the words, "I bless," and, "I curse," the words take on a life of their own. Job's curses are more than just venting. Like black magic, they aim to cause his hostile intentions to become reality.[3] Although he doesn't curse God, to end his misery he believes cursing his life will provoke God to crush him.

Even if you don't believe in the magical power of curses, perhaps the enormity of your disaster, the hopelessness of your life without your loved one, or your daily living with chronic physical pain, might make a curse seem to express your depth of despair. But before you give in to hopelessness, there is another way to express how you feel. In the second half of chapter 3, Job voices his feelings through lament.

ANOTHER OPTION

Why did I not die at birth, expire as I came forth from the womb?

Why does [God] give light to the sufferer ... to those who wait for death but it does not come? ... Whom God has hedged about? (Job 3:11, 20, 21, 23).

Why? Why? Why? Five times in the second half of chapter 3, Job asks questions similar to what we might ask: "Why didn't I die at birth? Why provide knees to receive me or breasts to suck? Why wasn't I stillborn? Why give life to someone whose soul is bitter, to a man who has no reason to live?" He concludes: "Why does He give life... to the man who has lost his way, whom God has hedged about?" (v. 23)[4] At some point, we also may have lamented, "Why me, God?"

In a lament, a believer pours out his anguished heart to God. When a believer feels separated from the living God, when she longs for reconnection with God and with God's power, she often prays a worshipful lament.[5] In his chapter 3 lament, however, Job offers no prayer of worship. Although his immediate responses to his tragedies reflect his submission—gestures of grief, words of realism, trust, and praise to God—here he explodes. As he unloads his despair on his friends, he transforms grief into complaint and sadness into curses. God imprisons him, he says, with unjust suffering. Trapped, he feels lost. "Why?" is his lamenting refrain.

When we experience tragedy, it's normal to feel lost. We struggle. We become confused about life, distraught with grief, and worried about the future. In a life of suffering, even Christians with deep faith can, at times, long to die. Have we never heard someone in misery say, "This isn't fair! I wish I were dead"? Have we never said it ourselves?

For years Juli and Paul prayed for relief. But relief never came. At times, it seemed God had forgotten them. To cope, they memorized part of Psalm 42: "Why have you forgotten me? Why do I go mourning because of the oppression of the enemy? As a shattering of my bones, my adversaries revile me, while they say to me all day long, 'Where is your God?'" Like many, Juli and Paul didn't understand God's purpose for their intense suffering. Would relief ever come? Why did God remain silent?

Perhaps you also struggle with chronic illness, a disabled child, or a handicapped marriage partner. *How long can I keep going?* you wonder. *When will it end? Will it end?*

When Job says, "whom God has hedged about," he holds God responsible for his tragedies. Most people recoil from the idea of God hedging in ("hemming in") Job or anyone with suffering. Some, however, like Mike after Katrina hit, have felt that way. Perhaps you also have questioned God for that reason.

Why did You do this to me?

You may want to know the reason for the unexpected death of your loved one, why you suddenly must bear the responsibility of caring for someone you love in chronic pain. You may feel God distant or unresponsive to your prayers. You may even hold God responsible for your changed circumstances. What can you do?

With a lament, you can express your deepest frustration with God—to God. When you don't feel you can contain your emotional pain; when, because of the toll of your suffering, you feel separated from God; when you long for that sweet fellowship again—with Job you can move from curses into lament. You can lament how distant God seems, how unresponsive to your prayer, how silent to your pleas for relief. Lament the pointlessness of your suffering.

Job's lament expresses for all of us the cry of a broken heart; frustration when God doesn't intervene; and sometimes blind, raging curses for a life of misery. Even if we don't harm ourselves, we may entertain questions about the point of our living. Although we may want to die, however, we can choose not to.

It's Our Choice

"I am really, really sorry, Pete." Peter recognized the neighbor friend who had just opened his garage door, but seeing the two police officers, one on her right, the other on her left, worried him. *O Man, I'm going to spend the night in a seventy-two hour hold,* he thought. Although he reassured them he was okay, he wasn't and visited his garage once more that evening. Nevertheless, after that dress rehearsal, he says, "I didn't attempt it again. I decided not to stay in a dark place."

In that friend's intervention, Peter saw "an incredible demonstration of love. She took that risk, and I told her and her husband how significant that was for me. She touched my heart."

SIGNS OF PROGRESS

Job also weathers his crisis. Although he concludes most of his dialogue speeches with his friends on the theme of death, he articulates many other thoughts. In his speech of chapters 6 and 7, for example, he also defends his innocence, castigates his friends for not believing him, bemoans human hardship, and addresses God about His harassment. Although thoughts of death never leave his mind, Job begins a long, slow process back toward living.

Job's almost imperceptible drift from his desire to die provides two major lessons for us. First, we may not at first detect signs of progress. Observing someone from the outside, we can miss early evidence of recovery. A cursory reading of Job may lead us to believe he's not making any progress at all.

TIME TO OVERCOME

Second, if we struggle with thoughts of wanting to die, we can overcome them—but not all at once. We will need time. We will think about other things for a while, only to revert to our depressed mood, or perhaps our wish to die. Over time, however, we will find ourselves focused more on thoughts of life and living, and less on thoughts of death, particularly if we find consistent support.

In my own family, some of those sources of support helped Juli survive. Her relationship with God continues strong, a sign of hope. The passage from Psalm Forty-two, which Paul and Juli memorized, concludes: "Hope in God, for I shall yet praise Him, the help of my countenance and my God." As he addresses his own soul, the psalmist says in effect, "Put your hope in God. I may not be able to praise Him now, nor for a good long time, but I shall yet praise Him." Juli has put her hope in God. She spent many years memorizing Scripture, listening to sermons, and watching DVDs of Bible teaching. All of those steps strengthened her faith.

I wish I could describe the miracle of Juli's physical healing, but I can't because she hasn't been healed. She remains severely limited, in pain, and in constant need of assistance. But she continues to trust in God for help and deliverance.

Job could have chosen death but instead he chose life. What helped him? We note the role of his family, friends, and God. Job sees none of the solutions he receives from these as perfect, yet each provides him needed support to transform his tragedies. Because of his friends' support, he can express his deepest anguish and pursue life. Although they deeply misunderstand him, his friends nevertheless stick by him. Even though Job's wife questions his claimed innocence in chapter 2, she remains with him. His brothers and sisters, mentioned only in chapter 42, provide family consolation later.

For Job, God at this point represents an ambivalent experience. Despite Job and his culture's interpretation of tragedy as sent from God to punish sin, Job knows his own innocence. He therefore protests. In pursuit of vindication, Job also pursues God—a first-hand, face-to-face confrontation. And he gets his wish! That longing for a confrontation with God also helps keep Job alive. At the end of Job's story in chapter 42, we find all three present: his wife, friends, and God.

How Do I
Live With Wanting to Die?

If you've experienced tragedy, no advice from a book will fully satisfy, but here are a few suggestions you may find helpful:

1. Talk about how you feel. With so much popular psychology and counseling in our culture, that may sound trite. But because of your own comfort level or through what you may think others expect, you may feel you must control your feelings. I encourage you to find a trusted friend or pastor with whom to share your deepest grief.

2. Read the five chapters of the Bible book Lamentations, then write your own lament to God. We seldom think today of lamentation as a way to express our grief, but it is both biblical and effective. Recall Jeremiah's poignant refrain over Jerusalem's destruction, "There is none to comfort her" (chapter 1). Walter C. Kaiser, Jr., an Old Testament scholar, says the book of Lamentations, instead of answers or slogans, "supplies (1) orientation, (2) a voice for working completely through grief (from *a* to *z*), (3) instruction on how and what to pray, (4) a focal point in God's faithfulness and in the fact that He is our portion."[6] Take a blank piece of paper or use your journal to jot down what you most miss. You may write only two or three sentences, or you may write and write. Don't change, correct, or cross out: let it flow. When you've finished, you may want to keep it locked up forever, or, like a Fifth Step in Alcoholics Anonymous, simply ask a trusted friend to hear it without comment or discussion. In a time of difficulty, your lament to God can provide a useful tool.

3. Assess your mood. Perhaps the most helpful step we can take after tragedy, loss, or trauma is to assess if, and how seriously, we feel depressed. We need to assess whether our feelings warrant the attention of a professional. According to some experts, after the death of a spouse, in normal bereavement, sadness begins to lift within two months. Others believe two months is too short a time. If your sadness continues much longer, however, you may ask yourself these important questions:

1.) Am I in a depressed mood (sad, crying) most every day?

2.) Have I lost interest in life or joy in life?

3.) Do I sleep too much or too little?

4.) Do I have too little appetite, or do I overeat? Has there been significant change in my body weight?

5.) Do I lose concentration? Am I unable to make decisions?

6.) Am I tired? Do I experience a lack of energy daily?

7.) Do others say I move too slow or too fast physically from point A to point B?

8.) Do I feel guilty or worthless?

9.) Do I have recurring thoughts of death or suicide, with or without a specific plan for suicide? Have I attempted suicide before?[7]

If you experience five or more of these symptoms daily, you may have major depressive disorder and require both competent counseling and medication from a physician. Repeated studies show psychotherapy and medication together help more than either alone.

How Do I
Move On?

An analysis of Job's early recovery reveals slow, almost imperceptible progress. In his early dialogues with his friends, Job never completely leaves thoughts of death or the grave, but he lives on despite them. He argues, debates, listens, and protests. Yet he survives.

If you want to overcome your desire to die, here are steps you can take:

1. Talk about subjects other than how you feel. This does not deny your feelings, because they will keep coming back, but life makes other demands on you. As much as possible, resume your personal responsibilities. If you're unable to do that, you may need professional help. Job leaves thoughts of death slowly, but he does move on.

2. Busy yourself with other activities. You may feel hopeless at first, but you can refuse to allow those feelings to control what you do. Expect thoughts of death, dying, and depression to fade slowly. If they persist or intensify, you may need to find professional help.

3. Read portions of the Scriptures daily. They provide life-giving hope for people in all circumstances. You may find a daily devotional guide helpful. Spend time in meditation on what you read.

4. Read self-help books on overcoming depression.

5. Maintain good physical health: exercise, nutrition, and sleep.

6. Use support wherever you find it: family, friends, church, prayer group, doctor, or pastor. Listen to ministries on Christian radio and TV. They can support your recovery.

If thoughts of death or suicide persist, if you have experienced thoughts of self-harm before, or if you have made attempts at self-harm, report this to your primary care physician or counselor.

7. Pour out your heart to God and to someone who will listen. Good friends want to help. Trust them.

FACING OUR VULNERABILITY

In life, whether from natural disaster, violence from people, critical illness, or accident, we face uncertainty. To deal with many contingencies today, we take out insurance. But no amount of insurance, planning, or anticipation of what could happen can prepare us for the reality of what does.

To acknowledge our vulnerability enables us to avoid an unwarranted assumption about tragedy: we can't prevent everything. When tragedy strikes, we're left with a lot of grief, emptiness, and questions about how we'll make it. We also have a lot of hurt to work through. Mike, Andrea, and Peter struggled with some of those emotions. So did Job.

Here we see Job the victim of disaster after disaster. We remember him that way—the helpless victim of forces of nature and of violent people. But there is much more to his story. In fact, observing how Job recovers can encourage you as you rebuild your life. That's where we'll go next in our discussion.

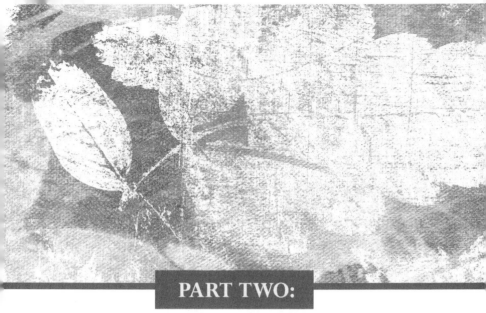

PART TWO

RECOVERY— STEPS TOWARD TRANSFORMATION

FROM DESPAIR TO RECOVERY

CHAPTER 5

SUE THE CULPRIT!

I F, AFTER TRAGEDY, we survive the wish to die, we may feel angry.

After a parishioner who'd been a good friend died, I entertained and quickly suppressed the thought, *How could you go and die on me?* His dying, of course, had nothing to do with me, but I, angry at my loss, experience it as if it had. If we've experienced loss, anger is an emotion that is likely to overtake us. Only with great reluctance do we give up what we feel is ours. That applies to more than possessions. Even if we expect it, when we lose a loved one we can feel angry over the loss of a cherished relationship.

It's unfair to lose so much, or to hurt so much. Maybe others' mistakes or negligence created the loss we feel. Or perhaps, like with Mike and Andrea, a natural disaster caused it. Through no fault of our own, we're left with years of work to recover. In some ways we may never fully recover.

A friend visited my wife and me at our summer cottage. She was a permanent resident in the area and a

47

leader in her community. She joined us at our picnic table on our screened-in porch with a view of a small lake.

"I'm a rape victim," she said. Our faces registered surprise at her vulnerable announcement. We had been talking about loss. She continued by telling us that in an attempt to facilitate recovery, she fought traumatic stress symptoms through mental health treatment for many years. Hearing her emotional pain made me think of the many thousands of people with hidden scars, people who quietly struggle to overcome a traumatic loss of innocence, of secret violence against them.

Some, perhaps most, feel the urge for revenge, borne out of righteous anger allowed to fester.

You may live with some of those same feelings. Because of how others traumatized you, you climb a mountain of serious illness, run to stand still on a treadmill of mental disability, or fight against depression strong enough to threaten your life. Your story resembles many others'.

Sadly, many people with abusive, neglectful and/or dysfunctional family experiences direct anger toward themselves. As a result they live with serious physical and mental health consequences.

ANGER AGAINST OURSELVES

The San Diego Kaiser Permanente Department of Preventive Medicine, along with the national Centers for Disease Control (CDC), analyzed the effect of Adverse Childhood Experiences (ACE) on 17,000 people.[1] Researchers examined ten categories: recurrent physical abuse (beatings, not mere spanking); contact sexual abuse; a member of household abused drugs or alcohol; a member of household incarcerated; a member of household chronically depressed, mentally ill, institutionalized, or suicidal; mother treated violently; not raised by both biological parents; physical neglect; emotional neglect. They then compared the frequency of such experiences with later wellbeing: social function, health risks, disease, healthcare costs, and life expectancy. Fifty years after those traumatic events, the study matched the person's current state of health and wellbeing against their ACE score. Researchers then followed up with a record of doctor's office visits, emergency room use, hospitalization, pharmacy costs, and death

Results revealed the strong relationship between increasing ACE scores and chronic depression in men and women in later life. This pattern also holds for other serious mental and physical health problems: suicide attempts, rates of anti-depressant prescriptions, hallucinations, impaired childhood memories, smoking, alcoholism, IV drug use, increased number of sexual partners (greater than fifty), chronic obstructive pulmonary disease (COPD), and coronary artery disease. The researchers also found a correlation between increased ACE scores and increased healthcare costs and decreased life expectancy.

People tend to respond to early injustice with life-long self-destructive tendencies. It's as if they tell themselves, *If I can't make someone else pay, my body will.* Those tendencies represent an enormous cost to the people involved, to their loved ones, and to society.

ANGER AGAINST OTHERS

Self-directed anger represents only one way people strike back against injustice. Another way is to seek justice by focusing our anger on others. One of the most public of those ways is through the courts.

In Karen Koehler's guest blog, fellow trial lawyer David Ball identifies the main reasons why he has seen people sue. The two most prevalent motives are the need to seek closure (he calls it *completion*), and the need to make something good out of something bad. Closure represents our human need to enable recovery; to make something good out of bad reflects our need for transformation.

Closure

In seeking closure, the offended party needs to know "the other shoe has dropped." In some way people need to find resolution, whether through apology, remorse, revenge, or punishment the person who sues will find satisfying.

"The drive for the other shoe to drop," Ball says, "is one of the strongest drives we have—because it is a survival necessity…Needing the other shoe to drop is common to all human beings, and hence common to everyone who sues." By *survival necessity*, Ball means a society or individual who refuses to right a wrong encourages further wrongs and threatens their survival. "If you wrong me and I do nothing about it, I am in greater danger of you wronging me again."

Part of this need, too, is for the wronged individual to prevent the same harm to others. "This drive is astonishingly common among plaintiffs," he says.

Make Things Good

To sue also derives from the human need to bring something good from the bad. "We have an automatic, unconscious, almost irresistible, drive," Ball says, "to turn catastrophe into something good." Here he listed as examples Hurricane Katrina, new buildings after 9/11, and the saying, "The only thing wrong with being knocked down is not getting up again." He sees this evidenced after every great community/national disaster.[2]

The need to heal relates closely to our need to recover, to establish normalcy, even if that involves a new normal. Our desire to bring about justice also derives from our need to bring redemption out of our tragedy, to help others even if our own loss is irreparable.

How do you experience the sense of injustice? Do you feel the need for closure? Do you also want to see your tragedy transformed into something good? If so, your need is not unusual.

ANGRY—WITH GOD?

There is one other place we may focus our anger—God. Because of the destructive potential to our health and relationships, when we experience injustice, rather than focus our anger on ourselves or on others, it is better in some cases to focus at least some of our anger on God.

Because of guilt, shame, or theology, we resist admitting we feel angry with God. We would rather blame others or ourselves, than the all-loving God we worship. He has also blessed us in many ways. But that was before tragedy. Now we still want to worship, praise, and experience God's fellowship, but we can't. How can we trust someone who allows us to suffer? We don't like to think those thoughts, but there we are—mad—at God. It isn't fair! I know the feeling.

"Why?" Each Sunday with tears I choked back the question.

In line of sight of the piano and pulpit, from where my wife and I usually worshipped, I watched Bill. A young, talented pianist, he honored the Lord with beautiful music as he accompanied our singing. But I couldn't appreciate his ministry.

Why? Why, when our son Paul is just as talented, just as committed, why isn't he playing? I asked. *Why is he sick, incapacitated, and lying in bed? God, How could you do this?* Not only Juli, but Paul, too, had spent years in bed with chronic fatigue syndrome. God was unfair; I felt angry.

Immediately after his losses, Job still worships and praises God. But the passage of time allows the enormity of those losses to sink in. For him, as for many people today, life is misery, and God is responsible. Because he can't find any sin he has committed to deserve his massive losses, he believes he has cause to feel angry with God:

> *Why do you hide your face and treat me as your enemy?*
> *('oyeb) (Job 13:24).*

Job and *enemy* represented by the transliterated words in English *'oyeb* (enemy) and *'iyyob* (Job), sound similar in Hebrew. By the selection of his name, therefore, the author infers Job and God might become enemies. Given the enormity of his losses, Job could have taken his life. Instead, he takes two steps to deal with his crisis: He complains of injustice and sues the culprit.

LIFE'S NOT FAIR!

Truly man has a term of service on earth; his days are like those of a hireling—
Like a slave who longs for evening's shadows, like a hireling who waits for his wage. So have I been allotted months of futility; nights of misery have been apportioned to me (Job 7:1-3).

In chapter 7, Job levels a broadside against God's justice. Not only Job, but also all people live "months of futility" and "nights of misery." That, says Job, means slavery. God gives Job a life of sleeplessness, broken and festering skin, days speeding by like a weaver's shuttle ending "when the thread runs out," i.e., without hope.[3] Job's life is short "as a cloud fades away," headed for the grave from which there is no return.

Because his life is short, he believes he has nothing to lose if he puts his anger with God into words. "I will not speak with restraint, but give voice to the anguish of my spirit and complain in the bitterness of my soul." Job feels angry with God for his miserable life, for God's unspeakable, sadistic treatment. So he fights back.

We tend to gloss over these statements. We don't want to see what Job really says, but Job's angry outbursts serve an important function. With his honest expression of intense anger with his life, with his friends—and with God, he backs away from his desire to die. To call God to account Job has to live.

Job is not the only servant of God who expresses anger with

God. You may recognize Joni Eareckson Tada, who has become known worldwide for her ministry to the disabled. But you may not know that a couple of years after the diving accident that left her quadriplegic, Joni complained bitterly to God. When her hockey-playing friend Jacqui cheered her with unrealistic expectations of recovery, Joni balked.

"I was tired of waiting...of urinating through a tube and defecating in bed, [of] smelling my matted hair and watching TV sideways. I was weary of *The Price Is Right* and soap operas, of eating lying down and being 'up' for interns on their morning rounds." She was desperate to reassure visitors she was getting better in answer to their prayers, yet even her medication-blackened teeth betrayed her true condition because it marred her smile. As the seasons passed in her hospital bed, Joni's angry thoughts, like Job's, focused on the culprit.

> *What's going on, God? Why aren't I getting better? God, You can't do this.*

Much as Job did during his week of silence in chapter 2, Joni lay prostrate for years, paralyzed from the neck down, with time to think and to feel. She felt like she was God's guinea pig.

"What is the meaning of life, *God?*" Joni hissed. "Do you bring people into this world just to breathe, eat, grow old, and die? Do you toss the dice and paralyze people along the way? Or throw in a little cancer? Or smash some brains in an accident? *Huh?*"[4]

Joni's fury at God, like Job's, seems to know no bounds.

Although uncomfortable for people around us to hear, a believer's angry words may be a necessary step toward recovery. They provide hope we are not alone, express our honest feelings to God, and (as with marriage partners) in the end promote intimacy through speaking the truth. Without that expression of honest rebellion against God for our plight, anger can turn to intensified depression or bitter resentment. Like with Job our anger may, in fact, represent a source of strength.

Angry at his miserable life, Job focuses his anger on the One he sees as his real enemy—God. Because God wronged him, he will no longer remain silent. Job protests his life in the presence of a small group of colleagues, wisdom teachers like he used to be. Although he speaks a soliloquy on his meaningless life, he does so, not in splendid isolation, but with his friends. His friends, however, have ideas of their own about Job's suffering—and his protest.

Eliphaz, the first to speak, responds in chapter 4 with the kindness befitting his role as elder of the group. While he also provides Job with a revelation to answer Job's concerns, with advice as to what he, Eliphaz, would do, Job's earlier ferocious attack on God triggers a confrontation over Job's anger.

"Vexation kills the fool," says Eliphaz in chapter 5, "passion slays the simpleton." With this proverb, Eliphaz alerts Job to the danger of his impassioned curses on his life. Although Eliphaz doesn't directly accuse Job of being a "fool" (in biblical terms, morally corrupt), he worries. Like the defendant whose outburst in court harms his case, Job's outburst against his life, Eliphaz fears, carries with it the potential to lead Job to a bad end. Perhaps Job will, with Eliphaz's help, become aware of his danger and self-correct—calm himself.[5] Eliphaz, however, like many people, misunderstands Job's anger.

"If my anguish were weighed," Job responds in chapter 6, "my full calamity laid on the scales, it would be heavier than the sands of the sea; that is why I spoke recklessly." While Eliphaz sees Job's outburst as foolhardy anger (*ka'ash*, "vexation"), Job defines his emotion—he uses the same word (*ka'ash*, "anguish")—as justifiable righteous anger.[6] "The arrows of the Almighty are in me," says Job in chapter 6. As a result of God's hostility, he has lost his wealth, businesses, employees, children, health, and, perhaps, even his wife's confidence. Anguish as heavy as "the sands of the sea" weigh him down, therefore, to the point of hopelessness.

People may also misunderstand our anger with God. Our friends may rush to God's defense, want us to tone down our justifiable outrage, or shame us into concealing it. "You know you didn't mean that."

With Eliphaz (and eventually all three friends) defending God against Job's accusations of injustice, where will Job go with his anguish? If his friends reject Job's words of protest, even finding in them evidence of guilt, how will Job express the depth of his suffering? Although he later speaks choice words about his companions' lack of true friendship, Job trains his biggest guns on the real culprit—God.

In chapter 3 Job speaks, something he couldn't do for a week. In severe depression, he mobilizes his meager resources to let loose with what he thinks and feels. Like a tormented bull, Job's anger toward God remains, at times hidden, at times open. For Job to articulate that anger, however, brings him out of his silent depression. Because in depression we direct anger against ourselves, Job's unexpressed anger could lead to suicide. To express anger toward God, therefore, provides a safer target, away from self.

You also may feel angry with God for the injustices in your life. Angry with Him for how He allowed others to abuse, neglect, or cause you trauma. You may not know what to do with your anger, except to hide it, even from yourself. If so, Job's example of protest can provide a healthy model for speaking up. It may also reassure us that God accepts our expression of our true human feelings. In fact, Job takes his case a step further. To resolve his outrage at injustice, Job develops a plan.

JOB'S PLAN—SUE THE CULPRIT

Indeed I know that it is so: man cannot win a suit against God. If he insisted on a trial with Him, He would not answer one charge in a thousand (Job 9:2-3).

To obtain justice, Job decides to sue. He develops the idea slowly. In chapter 4 Eliphaz shares with Job his revelation: "Can mortals be acquitted by God?" Because humans are mortal, says Eliphaz, they are therefore sinful.

Bildad, Job's second friend, in chapter 8 also asks the rhetorical question, "Will the Almighty pervert justice?"

In response, Job reflects at length on the implication of those questions and the terms *acquitted* and *justice.*

At first, in chapter 9 Job interprets his friends' questions in the legal sense, of a lawsuit. He then quickly discounts that possibility. "Indeed, I know that it is so: Man cannot win a suit against God," he says. He nevertheless explores what such a suit would involve: Could he, Job, win? Would God answer Job's charges? Would God strike Job back? If Job abandons his complaint, would he not still remain "in dread of all my suffering"? Even then, "I know that You will not acquit me," he says, addressing God (v. 28). Job then explores the possibility of an arbiter to provide a fair hearing.

With nothing to lose, in chapter 10 Job warms to the idea of a lawsuit, "I am disgusted with life; I will give rein to my complaint, speak in the bitterness of my soul." He then challenges God to "let me know with what You charge me." Job's lawsuit proceeds through a possible posthumous witness, a next-of-kin to defend Job's good name in chapter 19.[7] It climaxes with an all-out challenge at the conclusion of chapter 31: "O that [God] would reply to my writ, or my accuser draw up a true bill!" With a written *affidavit* Job pushes his advantage (i.e., his innocence of wrongdoing) to the point of no return. God must respond, Job thinks.

If, on the one hand, God brings no charges against Job: "Case dismissed." If, on the other hand, Job *has* sinned, at least his misery ends—quickly.

While the idea of a lawsuit against God may at first shock us, Job's speech is replete with legal terms.[8] Of more practical relevance for us today is Job's transformation from a passive victim to an active challenger. To sue God draws Job away from his self-destructive longing for death. It enables him to form a plan (however temporary) to take charge of his life, to accept responsibility for his sufferings, and to deal with God face to face. Facing God down may appeal to few of us today. But Job's example of taking charge of his life with all its losses, limitations, disabilities, and griefs challenges us to take responsibility for our life now.

ANGER—GOD'S GIFT

If God accepts Job's anger, why do many Christians forbid it? Christian psychologist Richard Butman, for example, writes, "Many, especially conservative Protestant Christians, have been explicitly taught that anger is a sin and should be avoided at all costs."[9] What is the purpose of anger? Anger, an intense emotional reaction, may prepare us for aggression.[10] That response to real or perceived threat promotes our survival.

"If we didn't have anger, we'd be like jellyfish, with no backbone," Rev. Kenneth Lloyd Garrison, a mentor early in my ministry, once told me. Triggered by a real stressor or a perceived threat, anger—an essential emotion—produces a chemical response in the brain. Under normal conditions, we process anger through our neo-cortex, the thinking part. We modify or redirect our actions, therefore, according to what our mind tells us makes sense. Under extreme duress, however, that rational response to a threat short-circuits. In perceived life-or-death circumstances, prior to reaching the neo-cortex, the impulse instantly transforms into an emotional fight/flight response. That enables us to defend to the death or to escape with our life.[11]

When Job curses his life, he wants to die by God's hand. His response to his losses, however, leads him into depression. One major component of depression is sadness; another is anger. Job redirects his anger away from himself to a counterattack against God for his injustice—he will fight. In the same way Job's death wish in chapter 3 shocks us (especially if we have little personal experience with depression), his angry words against God may also come as a shock.

Looked at as the honest expression of a person in despair, however, Job's anger with God provides hope. In fact, constructive expression of anger contains the potential to deepen and enhance a relationship.[12] Job's agenda to confront God differs from his wife's and his friends'. His spiritual resources, too, were greater than we or he might have anticipated. His once-vital relationship with God leads him to seek an audience with God, to welcome a confrontation, and to invite God's charges against him. Job's ability to put his feelings into words—and act—represents a source of strength.

This is also true of us. Depressed, angry, focused on what we lost during periods of testing, we minimize our strengths, resources, and support. But, like Job we have a mind of our own, a sense of what will help us. If God is or has been real to us, we can petition Him to be heard, lament our losses, express our true feelings, and expect a response. As with Job, however, that response may not come when or how we expect. We may find comfort in learning that others, even Bible saints, felt the same way.

How Do I
Live With My Anger?

1. Feeling angry about your loss is normal. Since it's not a sin, can you accept your anger with God? Find someone to hear your anger, to listen without comment, question, or advice. Tell God, "I feel angry with You." Pinpoint the focus of your anger with God. If you can use words to express your anger with God, you may find it dissipates more quickly than it would otherwise.

2. Read Job's speeches aloud. Observe his anger with God: direct, focused, and clearly articulated. Can you identify with his emotion? It leads to concrete action. "I insist on arguing [my case] with God," Job says. The lesson: Speak up! Say what you feel. Take action! For a time Job couldn't speak, but as soon as he could, he did!

3. Your expression of angry feelings needn't be harsh. There is a gentle way to express even deep anger: "I love you and I need you, but I'm very hurt and feeling angry right now. Could we talk about it?" Your anger at an undeniable tragedy is appropriately expressed by directing it to the One In Charge. As Joni Eareckson Tada prayed, "God, I don't much like you, I'm not happy with you, but you know what? I don't have anywhere else to go; I don't know who else to turn to."[13]

4. Rethink your idea of God. To his friends, Job's anger was a sure sign that he was hiding some secret sin for which he was being punished. But that was not God's view. Big enough to contain Job's anger, God is big enough to contain yours. When we can honestly express our anger with God, we have begun our recovery.

5. Constructive expression of anger involves accepting how you feel, exploring the reason, respecting the other person, and a making a commitment to maintain the relationship.[14] That was borne out in Job's relationship with God.

How Do I
Move on From My Anger?

1. Work it through. In psychotherapy, *working though* describes the major work of the client or patient. He or she makes repeated attempts to use insight, the connection between present feelings and past events. "[Working through] is the client's trying out a new way of looking at himself or herself in a variety of relationships and experiences."[15] The *working-through* process is slow, sometimes painfully so, as the individual tries, fails, and tries again to gain mastery over their emotions. With practice, however, the client gradually improves his or her ability to integrate insight, reduce anxiety, and form healthier relationships.

2. Share how you feel with a small group or trusted friends. Seek out others who have experienced losses similar to yours. Find support groups through local churches, mental health and community service agencies.

3. Establish a regular time of reflection, meditation, or devotion. Many Psalms express feelings similar to yours, including feeling angry with God. Observe how the Psalmist expresses his feelings and how he then returns to the theme of trust in God.

CHAPTER 6

AM I CRAZY?

W E RESPOND TO the stress of a crisis in different ways. Some of us cling to what we know. Others explode in rage against people, even God, for His failure, perceived or real, to prevent our tragedy. We can also give up in despair, wishing for death. Job at different times responded in each of those ways.

Another possible response to the stress of tragedy, especially trauma, involves extreme fear. Many trauma victims experience heightened alertness, increased vigilance, and recurring images and nightmares of the original traumatic events. The paranoid person lives with constant fear of others' hostility, especially authority figures. Paranoia, from two words meaning *beside* and *mind,* describes fear to the extreme.

Consider, for example, Carl Johnson's dream.

> *Our whole family was at the beach. I reached*
> *down into the water and picked up a rock, a piece*
> *of petrified wood with strong-looking hieroglyphics.*
> *Immediately, I had this doubt: I was worth-*
> *less, stupid, crummy, messed up. The whole family*

attacked me, total condemnation: "You're absolutely worthless.
There's nothing you can do about it."
  "See, I told you so," my dad said.
  Right at the end, only mom was left. Everyone else had gone.
  "In about one-and-a half hours you're going to hell," she
said. "Our whole family is going to hell."
  I started screaming, screaming, screaming.

Carl's screams woke him. "This is a disaster," he said. "That
was the most vicious dream I've had in my life." Carl's dream of
abandonment and condemnation would scare most people.

Prior to counseling, Carl used hallucinogenic drugs and mari-
juana. After using those drugs he said, "I had thoughts I couldn't
get out of my head."

Carl thought co-workers didn't like him; he also felt the
bosses upstairs harassed him. When he asked his co-workers if
they were talking about him, they denied it, but their denials
only temporarily reduced his suspicions.

Carl's thinking distracted him. "I'm always behind in my work,
because I think too much," Carl said. "So I have to work through
my lunch hour to make up the time." Repeatedly Carl checked to
see if he had turned off the lights and gas, and locked the doors.

"I got fired from my job after I caused an accident and didn't
report it. That was actually the third time."

Yet, Carl is a Christian and, through most of his eleven years
in counseling, attended a Bible-preaching congregation. "I like
my pastor, but I always thought he preached against me. I would
ask him after each service and he acted surprised, and said no."
Carl also regularly attended a men's prayer group. Because Carl
received Christ at a Billy Graham crusade, underwent baptism,
and attended church regularly, you might think he would be able
to deal with his life. In fact, his many problems caused friends to
accuse Carl of not having enough faith. But he also believed that

if he would just let go and trust God, he wouldn't have these difficulties. His story prevents us from offering simple solutions.

The person with paranoid fear feels uncontrollable rage, but experiences it as if it comes from other people: I am not angry with you (denial); you are out to get me (projection). By blaming or attributing to others what we feel, we project our feelings onto others.

"I was driving here today," Carl told his counselor, "going 50 – 60 mph. on a gravel highway. A guy tailgated me. I felt guilty about feeling so angry, so I prayed to God to forgive me for my obnoxious behavior."

"I felt murderously angry at the man," he said later. "But I was worried about how I would do in a fight. When I saw the man drove a government car, I felt guilty. I was afraid he might report me."

Carl worked with his counselor to identify the specific thoughts that triggered negative feelings about himself. He harbored fears of being less than fully masculine. In his mind, therefore, he is defective, the reason God punishes him, not simply for having done wrong (guilt), but because he is a bad person. Carl experiences shame. If Carl *is* bad, what can he do to overcome his weakness, defect or sin? Nothing. Tragically, he believes he is truly worthless, deserving only God's punishment. Throughout his counseling, Carl met with a psychiatrist and used prescribed medications to manage his symptoms. In addition, he met with an employment counselor and, for a time, entered drug rehabilitation.

Like Carl, you also may struggle with a mental disorder. Being a Christian or a person of strong faith did not prevent you from mental illness, perhaps life-long. Many people view the mentally ill as spiritually immature, lacking faith, or someone who won't trust God. They may also feel you shouldn't depend on "drugs." Much like living with a physical handicap, such as a broken leg, you live with a "limp," this one emotional.

Five Hostile Images of God

In the same way Carl's Christian faith did not prevent him from experiencing diagnosable mental disorders, Job's faith did not prevent the effects of traumas, traumas that lead him to the borderline of mental illness. Like many people who have experienced trauma, Job knows terror. In his case, those terrors focus on God. In his debates with his colleagues, Job uses five hostile images to describe his experience with God. In his first response to his fellow wisdom teacher Eliphaz, Job reveals his first hostile image of God—the Heavenly Archer.[1]

The Heavenly Archer

> *For the arrows of the Almighty are in me, my spirit drinks*
> *their poison. God's terrors are arrayed against me (Job 6:4).*

Eliphaz had told Job that suffering results from personal sin, from disease from Reshef, god of pestilence, and from God's discipline. Through his arrows Reshef "the archer," introduces disease.[2] "Happy is the man whom God reproves," Eliphaz says, so Job should welcome the discipline of the Almighty.

For Job, however, the enormity of his suffering prevents easy dismissal. He listens to Eliphaz, but rejects his rational explanations, ignores his advice, temporarily, to lay his case before God, and asserts the weightiness of his own suffering. "If my anguish were weighed...it would be heavier than the sands of the sea," Job says in chapter 6. Countering his friend, Job says his sufferings come instead from his murderous divine Enemy. Deadly accurate, poison-tipped arrows found their target: Job will soon die. "He set me up as His target; His bowmen surrounded me; He pierced my kidneys: He showed no mercy; He spilled my bile onto the ground," Job adds in chapter 16.

In chapter 6, Job pictures himself hanging wounded, poisoned, helpless, and dying. He longs to confront God to learn the reason for his suffering, yet experiences only divine terror. However well-intentioned and considerate, Eliphaz's rational explanations fail to account for Job's experience of massive loss or for his anger. While the image of God as the hostile Heavenly Archer is blasphemy to Job's friends, and, perhaps to us, it is a clue to understanding Job's suffering: his uncontained rage overflows, spilling over into paranoia.

When our massive losses pile up unrelentingly, we may conclude that God is against us. In denial of our anger with God, we blame Him, project our hostility onto Him, and fear His retaliation. If our suffering seems undeserved and extreme, we may feel paranoid fear. Angered by our loss, we may feel terrified of the God we once loved and served. Like Job, we may also feel God continually harasses us.

The Eye in the Sky

> *The eye that gazes on me will not see me; Your eye will seek me, but I shall be gone (Job 7:8).*

Job complains of humans' hard service on earth, his own sleepless nights, his skin disease, and the brevity of life. He feels hopeless. "Consider that my life is but wind," he tells God in 7:7, "I shall never see happiness again." Here he asks God to note the fragility of his life and the depth of his depression. He uses his own certain death, in fact, to goad God to respond: "Don't worry, I won't be around much longer, so speak up!" In the process of these complaints, Job reveals another way he experiences God—as a harassing Eye.

Other Scriptures describe God as One who observes and scrutinizes the lives both of saints and sinners. Psalm 11:4 says, for example, "The Lord is in his holy temple; the Lord is on his heavenly throne. He observes the sons of men; his eyes examine them"

(NIV). Job turns God's omniscience into a massive, hostile, divine CIA, FBI, KGB, and Homeland Security surveillance operation. We recall the introduction to Job's story, in which Satan plays the role of spy. Later in the same chapter, he addresses God. "Will you not look away from me for a while; let me be 'till I swallow my spittle? If I have sinned, what have I done to You, Watcher of men? Why make of me Your target, and a burden to myself?" Job's hostile caricature of God's all-seeing and all-knowing omniscience, challenges God's incessant, aggressive spying.

Perhaps you also have experienced an overactive God-consciousness, where God does nothing but watch your every move to catch you in some misstep. Maybe you're living with hostile attacks of guilt or shame for something not your fault. What can you do? Job gives us a clue.

In 6:4 Job expresses his fear of God's arrows to his friends, but in chapters 7 and 9 he takes another important step toward healing: he addresses God directly. "What is man that *You*...fix Your attention upon him?" (9:17–18). He speaks *to* God, the object of his fear. When you're terrified of someone, you may feel it impossible to express how angry you feel—to him or to her. That may be part of the price of Job's recovery, however, to put his most angry feelings into words, and then to address them directly to God.

Paranoid fear rests on the need to deny one's own hostility and to project it onto another person. Because anger lies on a continuum with (unconscious) murderous rage, the paranoid person fears her anger. She needs to keep a tight rein. The intensity of anger feels so overwhelming she can't acknowledge it. With the image of God as the Heavenly Archer, Job asks, "Why make of me your target?" (projection). However, here, with the image of God as the Eye in the Sky, Job identifies and addresses God with his underlying hostility, expressed with sarcasm: "till I swallow my spittle." Job speaks up; Job speaks to God: "I'm deathly afraid of you!" The best way to keep paranoia in check, therefore, is the straightforward, honest, direct expression of hostility to the appropriate object: "I feel angry with you because..." Job begins to treat God with honesty, expressing to God, without projection, his true feelings.

Risky as it may feel, with Job you may need to express your anger, fear, and even rage to God directly. Instead of saying what you think you should say or feel, practice saying to Him what you *do* feel.

Job uses several additional images to describe God:

The Ravenous Lion

In addition to the Heavenly Archer and the Eye in the Sky, Job also describes God as The Ravenous Lion.

"Is it something to be proud of, to hunt me like a lion?" Job asks God in chapter 10. With stealth, famished lions hunt for food.

"In his anger he tears and persecutes me. He gnashes his teeth at me," Job says in chapter 16, using similar imagery. With bared teeth the hungry lion tears apart his prey, so with anger God tears and persecutes Job.

The Vicious Warrior

"I had been untroubled, and He broke me in pieces; He took me by the scruff and shattered me... He breached me, breach after breach; He rushed at me like a warrior," Job complains in chapter 16. As a victorious soldier subdues his conquered enemy warrior by dashing his head by the neck, or after repeatedly breaching his fortress, so God repeatedly breaches and dashes Job. In the soldier's repeated attacks on "untroubled" Job, we may hear echoes of Job's serene life before the succession of four disasters.[3]

The Besieging General

"He kindles his anger against me; He regards me as one of His foes. His troops advance together; they build their road toward me and encamp around my tent" (19:12). He pictures himself surrounded by God's besieging army. He describes his defenseless, pitiful condition, hiding in his flimsy "tent." Against this Commander, he is helpless, shattered, dying.

As with the Eye, where Job turns God's infinite knowledge on its head, so also does he here reverse the experience of God's power. Those fearful, threatening, violent images of God expose Job as helpless. "He snatches away; who can stop Him? Who can say to him, 'What are You doing?'" he says of God the Almighty (9:12). Against this God, Job lies helpless, shattered, besieged, and dying. Yet he continues to protest to his friends—and to God.

EXTREME EMOTIONS EXPRESSED

If Job felt such extreme emotions toward God, we may at times also entertain similar thoughts. On the one hand, with his attacks Job tries to provoke God into a confrontation so that he, Job, may learn the sin for which he is punished. God's silence frustrates him. On the other hand, God's silence also could mean that God listens patiently to Job's complaints, diatribes, and attacks without retaliation. God shows Job no hostility in return. That is a key response to someone whose fear reaches paranoid proportions. Any hostility in return for provocation only confirms what the paranoid person already "knows" (that you're against him) and will jeopardize your relationship.

If Job expresses such angry sentiments *about* God as, "The arrows of the Almighty are in me," and *to* God, "If I have sinned, what have I done to You, Watcher of men?" why do we hold back our complaints? If Job feels such extremes of fear toward God as to describe him in those violent images, why do we fear to express our honest emotions about Him and to Him? If Job experiences a relationship with God strong enough to allow him paranoid fear, what kind of relationship do we enjoy? If Job's paranoid thoughts never seemed to bother God, if his words never draw God's retaliation, then maybe I can be as honest as Job. If Job's thoughts bordered so closely on the edge of insanity, perhaps God understands me when I can't control my weird thoughts. If God listens to Job's hostile images of Him without rejection or retaliation, perhaps He also patiently listens to our greatest fears. No thought scares God, not even thoughts of people with mental illness.

When God fails to respond, Job assumes God has abandoned him. However, another interpretation is possible: with eternal patience God awaits the right moment. That's also true of us. When God is silent, we may assume God has abandoned us. We need to consider another possibility: God patiently waits for us to get real with Him, to become honest about how we feel, and for the right moment to respond.

Carl's Work in Counseling

"Carl," said his counselor, "whenever you feel angry with me, I want you to tell me. 'This is how I feel...I'm upset with you right now.'" Since paranoia involves denial of one's own anger and its projection onto others, whenever Carl's counselor sensed Carl felt angry with him, he encouraged Carl to express that anger directly, appropriately, and verbally. That seemed to defuse Carl's rage: it helped him to put his feeling into words. Carl's feelings of anger the counselor could accept; his suspicions of the counselor's motives he found more difficult.

"I've got something I want to say," Carl would say. To work with Carl, at each session, his counselor learned to negotiate a weekly contest of wills. Carl feared being controlled through his counselor directing the agenda. Usually, Carl had specific things he sought to remember and to present. At other times, however, when he was unable to say anything, his counselor learned to wait until he was ready.

"Don't interrupt me," Carl would say. Carl refused to allow interruptions through the whole fifty-minute session. Often he could not or would not leave the session on time, expressing hurt and rejection if asked to leave when his time was up. He would then ask for prayer for reassurance. Also hindering progress was his inability to remember from one session to the next what they had talked about in the previous session.

Even positive self-regard Carl interpreted with self-hatred. "If I succeed," he said, "I will lead others astray with my success." His "vicious" dream above reflects that fear: he would lead his family to hell.

"I've committed the unpardonable sin," Carl said as he brought the counselor the passage he found that week to condemn himself. His feelings of paranoia colored every Scripture he read. Carl interpreted the passage to confirm his worst doubts about himself: God condemned him to hell as a worthless human.

"Let's read the passage together and see if there's another way to look at it," the counselor would say. Counseling consisted of helping Carl work through his worst fears of God's personal rejection based on his understanding of that Scripture. The counselor helped him look at the context of the passage, and read the passage in a different light. The counselor also reassured him that his worst fears were not to be trusted. Carl's reassurance would last until the next time an upsetting event triggered feelings of rejection. Carl found it difficult to believe that such feelings were triggered by specific events with people in his life.

Whenever he began to feel good, he would become severely depressed. Not believing he deserved anything good from life or from God, unable to experience any genuine pleasure, overwhelmed with a sense of shame and inadequacy about himself, and dreading what he believed he deserved, he expected anything positive would be punished.

Carl's therapy helped relieve his intense, uncontrollable

suffering from his negative self-condemnation. Through therapy, he gained perspective: the viewpoint of someone he trusted could counter his twisted perceptions born of self-hatred. Despite the religiousness of these negative thoughts, they were not the product of his faith, but of his mental illness. We can also learn from Job about the need to understand mental illness and someone like Carl. Carl's thoughts were beyond his ability to control, even with constant psychiatric medication.

Carl's story reminds us of the possibilities of extremes of human responses to childhood vulnerabilities. Although Job was, generally, mentally healthy until his disastrous losses, Carl's mental challenges dated from his earliest years. Nevertheless, we can learn from Carl about Job's paranoia, the intensity of it, the negativity, and the inability of reason to dislodge his overwhelming fear. Carl's story also reminds us of the patience it takes to minister to someone in such dire straits, the need to avoid easy answers, but the complimentary need to be a faithful and trustworthy friend, whether as a member of the family, a therapist, or a brother or sister in Christ.

Celebrating Limited Achievement

Carl's work accomplished important goals, however limited. Through his work in therapy, he kept himself alive. That was no easy achievement because, at times he would become suicidal.

Carl's therapy also helped him keep paranoia and murderous rage under control, so that not only did he not he harm himself, he avoided harming anyone else.

In addition, maintaining a person in outpatient treatment, and out of the hospital whenever possible, also significantly reduces emotional suffering on clients and families. Carl's hospitalizations were minimal, once prior to counseling, and once while in counseling.

Eventually, Carl came to express this anger directly, appropriately, and verbally. That defused his rage. That also prevented the build-up of shame for feeling angry. Finally, for over ten years, Carl had a place to go with his weekly and daily struggles with his mind, where he could share his most intimate, strange, and difficult-to-manage paranoid fears, dreams, obsessions and compulsions. He experienced trust.

HOW TO
LIVE WITH FEAR

1. Distinguish the kind of fear you experience. Some fears
   come from a realistic assessment of legitimate danger
   (e.g., driving too fast); some fears derive from the normal
   process of living (e.g., of getting sick, or of death).
   Anxiety is a type of fear which, when mild, motivates us
   to get busy with our responsibilities in working, and in
   family life: we fear arriving late at work, or not earning
   enough money to support our family, so we're punctual
   and industrious. Anxiety like Carl's that's not control-
   lable by corrective action and grows without an obvious
   reason, may need professional attention. If you experience
   heightened vigilance, suspicion, and fears of others having
   the intent to harm you, look into this with a professional.

2. Learn to share your fears with a person you trust.
   Especially if you live with fearful thoughts of others
   harming you, finding that person will not be easy. Fear of
   closeness (and of being attacked) makes this process ten-
   tative and slow, with lots of testing, in which you divulge
   small bits of information and observe their response,
   before sharing more.

3. Share your fears with God in prayer, as Job did. Learn to
   confide to Him your inmost secrets.

4. Become part of a church or prayer group with Christian
   love, acceptance, and encouragement.

HOW TO
MOVE ON FROM FEAR

1. If you feel extreme fear (paranoia) you cannot control, you will need help from a therapist you can come to trust. Continuing to try on your own will probably remain unfruitful. Ask for help. You may need time to locate the right person.

2. Get used to the idea that you may need medication(s) to help you control your thoughts. Talk with your counselor or doctor about a referral to a psychiatrist for a medication evaluation. Then you can work with your counselor on your strategies for dealing with stress and on your spiritual disciplines to enable you to continue growing emotionally and spiritually.

3. Find a support group through your local mental-health services agency. You're not alone in your battle with your mind. Others may have found strategies that you can use.

4. Watch the movie, *A Beautiful Mind* (2001) with Russell Crowe playing the role of a world-class mathematician who overcame schizophrenia to win a Nobel Prize. In this true story, Crowe learns how to distinguish reality from hallucinations.

5. Read Scriptures on fear, from Psalms and Proverbs. Read biographies of Bible characters who faced overwhelming fears in their ministry to learn how they overcame their fears. Observe the role God plays. Note the many times in Scripture we find the injunction to "Fear not!" Using a concordance, look up each passage, and study it in context.

CHAPTER 7

WITH FRIENDS
LIKE YOU . . .

AFTER WE SURVIVE the initial despair from tragedy, friends may try to help. But because our tragedy at first seems beyond their strength or skills, they feel helpless. So even if they call, visit, or pray, by and large they leave us to professionals. The doctor performs emergency surgery, the psychiatrist prescribes medication, or the physical therapist enables us to walk again. But friends haven't been involved by word or action.

These friends may want to help; even feel compelled. One thing some believe they can do: provide a clear explanation of the reason for your tragedy. Their theory, both ancient and modern, can make sense out of what seems a senseless cascade of uncontrollable events. These friends know the root cause of our disaster.

WHEN FRIENDS DISAPPOINT

After surviving a mysterious illness, thirteen-year-old Jessica heard from one such friend.

"On a school trip to South America," Jessica says, lying

in her robe on the living room sofa unable to move normally, "I developed a mild flu. I felt stomach pain and feverish. I ached all over. So when I came home a week later, my doctor treated me for traveler's diarrhea. When that medicine ran out, however, I got worse."

"My head hurt and I felt drained," Jessica said. "After I developed a higher fever and my head hurt more, my doctor prescribed alternating Tylenol and Advil to reduce the fever." Instead, her fever rose.

"One night," Jessica says, "I woke up with a body rash. My whole body began to swell; my eyes swelled nearly shut."

"I think she's had an allergic reaction to the previous medication," the emergency room doctor said. "Here is Benadryl to take home with you." But even after her second trip to the ER that night, her fever continued to rise.

"I know a lot about that country," the infectious disease doctor at a local hospital told her primary care doctor the next day. "Get her to the hospital as soon as possible." The hospital gave Jessica's mother an appointment that day.

"With my fever of 105° and blood pressure of 40/0," says Jessica, "only quick action by the medical staff saved my life. They couldn't find a vein, so the Intensive Care Unit nurses put me on a stretcher, turned me upside down, and injected medication into the one place they could find—my jugular vein." To prevent further shutdown of her organs, they inserted another catheter through her left side to inject medicine directly into her heart. After a couple of days in ICU and a few more in the hospital, Jessica began a five-year recovery.

"If I didn't have God in my life at that time," Jessica said, "I might have committed suicide. It was so overwhelmingly bad at times, I probably wouldn't be here, except that I knew God has a plan for me." Jessica's relationship with God provided solid ground for her to survive. At home in bed, Jessica learned that Beth, mother of a school friend, called to visit.

"She's a nice person," Jessica said, "and, although I didn't feel well as usual, I felt excited. I never turn anyone away who will pray over me."

"God led me to come and tell you that you need to confess your sin," Beth said. "Once you confess your sin, you'll improve." After Beth's exhortation, she asked for permission to pray. Jessica agreed.

"Lord, help Jessica not be obstinate but willing to look inside herself," Beth prayed, "to realize the sin she has committed and to confess it before you, so she can finally be healed."

Maybe I did, because I know I haven't lived a perfect life, thought Jessica at first after Beth left, *but I don't think that was the reason.*

"I was in shock," Jessica said, "ashamed to think God was mad at me. Beth's prayer made me doubt myself; I didn't think I did anything wrong. Beth's accusation hurt so bad."

Like many well-meaning helpers, Beth connected sickness with sin: in her mind, Jessica's sin hindered her healing. Beth believed she could help Jessica find healing through exhorting her to confess. In the end, however, that assumption only intensified the shame and self-doubt Jessica already felt about her illness; it created more hurt.

"I cried and cried!" said Jessica. "I told my mom what happened and she felt so upset, so furious. We debated calling Beth but decided against it. Mom called our pastor."

"Let's look at someone who suffered greatly," Pastor Eric said, "yet did nothing to deserve what happened to him. Job's pain came not from a sin he had committed, but from Satan's desire to test his loyalty to God."

"I felt a bit better after Pastor Eric's visit," Jessica said. "I have forgiven Beth, and I know she meant well. It's interesting that when we think we've heard from God, it is just ourselves or Satan trying to wreak havoc. I will never forget that experience."[1]

Perhaps you have a friend like Beth. With a direct message from God, they think they can put their finger on your exact spiritual diagnosis: you're suffering the results of your sin. Like Jessica, at first you may not respond, but later, when you think back, you feel deeply hurt. Especially after you've examined yourself and you can't put your finger on any offense to God.

WHAT CAN YOU DO?

Here are some steps to help you cope with hurtful friends.

1. Like pastor Eric, we can turn to the book of Job. Some Scriptures, such as Deuteronomy and the prophets, teach punishment for sin, but it doesn't always hold. Hard experience reveals a painful lesson: when we do right, we may still suffer. As the book of Job teaches us, God is not bound by our tight formulas of virtue rewarded and evil punished.

2. Like Job, we can turn even more energetically toward God. Although suffering can drive us *from* God, we can also allow suffering to draw us *toward* Him. Job failed to maneuver God into responding when and how he wanted. In the end, however, God responded to Job personally and honored him.

3. When someone says that God has spoken to them about you, consider saying, "Well, Thank you. Maybe He will confirm that by speaking to me." Remember that God can speak to you directly just as well as to your friend.

Since Job's time, those friends haven't changed much. If you'd like to learn how to help others through a time of despair, grief, or uncertainty, you can benefit from a careful look at Job's friends. They teach us many lessons—mostly what *not to* say.

If we care about our friend or loved one, we would want to avoid adding more hurt. If we establish good rapport, we will greatly benefit our friend in distress. It also helps if we avoid the blunders of Job's friends.

What I Would Do

But I would resort to God; I would lay my case before God (Eliphaz, Job 5:8).

After Job's death-desiring monologue in chapter 3, his colleague Eliphaz speaks first. Older, more experienced, and wiser, he gives Job the best wisdom he can offer. Eliphaz responds with traditional wisdom teaching, which provides practical instructions for godly living. Throughout chapters 4–5, he gently warns, advises, and reassures Job. He attempts empathy, grants Job deference, and shares his personal experience.

In response to Job's plea for death, Eliphaz gently asks permission to speak. He then says he can't hold back and offers several key applications of wisdom to Job's case. One is particularly relevant. Awakened from a deep sleep, Eliphaz's whole body trembles. His hair stands on end as a gentle breeze glides past his face. A breeze, or was it a spirit? The word in Hebrew can be translated either way. "A form loomed before my eyes," he says. What could that mean?

"Can mortals be acquitted by God, can man be cleared by his Maker?" says the form. "If [God] cannot trust his own servants [i.e., his angels], how much less [can he trust] those who dwell in houses of clay..." the apparition asks. If God our Creator is pure, and if beings of an order higher than humans, such as the angels, are of lesser purity, how can people like Job, who belong to an order of being lower than angels, claim to be pure? Because people are mortal, argues Eliphaz, they are sinful, including Job. Job claims he suffers as an innocent, but Eliphaz believes there are no innocent persons.

Like Jessica's friend Beth, Eliphaz represents many who believe they receive the truth of God directly through an unforgettable overwhelming personal experience.[2] "I felt led from God to come over," Beth told her. "There is sin you need to confess."

As a colleague, Eliphaz wants to believe in Job's innocence. The wisdom doctrine that God always rewards the righteous and punishes the wicked, however, leads him to conclude that Job must be foolish, wicked, or cursed. If Job will only acknowledge his sin, then he can rest easy. Based on his revelation, Eliphaz advises: "But I would resort to God. I would lay my case before God" (5:8). His "but" is strong and emphatic so that his statement reads, "But if it were I, I..."[3] Like all mortals, Job is a sinner, so Eliphaz emphatically implores Job to plead for God's mercy.

What can we learn from Eliphaz? Without a lot of careful listening, without acknowledging the feeling of the sufferer, and without considering the effect of our words on them, we will find our supposed wisdom falls on deaf ears at best, or, as with Jessica, it wounds deeply. If the answers to Job's problems were so patently obvious as Eliphaz indicates, Job would have solved his difficulty long before that moment. But like Jessica, Job did nothing to warrant his suffering.

If we want to help others in tragedy, we will avoid Eliphaz's well-meaning blunders. Our experience, no matter how compelling, remains *our* experience—not the sufferer's. The first true help we can offer is patient, concerted listening. Be assured that anything we suggest either has been tried, or it's too soon to consider for the sufferer, or it is (or seems) impractical. After hearing Job's plea for death, Eliphaz may believe Job is ready to receive what he offers, but he talks rather than listens. Eliphaz needs to hear Job at a much deeper level.

Job's Response

If my anguish were weighed . . . it would be heavier than the sand of the sea (6:2-3).

As if Job doesn't hear Eliphaz's words of supposed comfort, he continues to complain of his misery. Job says his anguish is too enormous to measure. He insists he has reason to "bellow" about his friends' sickening "food," i.e., their counsel. He laments the betrayal of their friendship: "A despairing man should have the devotion of his friends, even though he forsakes the fear of the Almighty. But my brothers are as undependable as intermittent streams" (6:14-15). Job's friends are like a ravine in arid land; in the rainy season, the water gushes, but when the heat comes, a lonely wanderer looks in vain for water to survive. Job is that lonely wanderer.

To help someone in tragedy we must convey: "I understand." But simply saying "I understand how you feel," except in circumstances where we have experienced something similar, gives us away as someone who doesn't. It's better to remain honest about our feeling of helplessness, inadequacy, or inability to know what to say than to say something that creates additional pain.

Premature reassurance also conveys a lack of understanding; accusation of wrongdoing creates more hurt. When we observe others in tragedy from a distance, we seem to find it easy to judge. However, as we learn more, we must admit our ignorance. What we learn may lead us to admit our lack of compassion.

Job longs for some word of understanding from his friend. Despite Eliphaz's efforts at sympathetic and wise advice, Job feels no understanding. Perhaps because of that, or because of his depression, Job interprets the words Eliphaz uses as evidence of hostility and deception.[4] Like most of us, Job responds negatively to accusation of sin.

Perhaps his next friend Bildad can understand.

It's Their Own Fault!

> *Will God pervert the right? Will the Almighty pervert justice? If your sons sinned against Him, he dispatched them for their transgression (Bildad, Job 8:3–4).*

Like Eliphaz, Bildad believes God rewards the righteous and punishes the sinner. The answer to Job's loss of his family, therefore, is clear to him: "If your sons sinned against him, he dispatched them for their transgression" (8:4). When Bildad insinuates that Job's children died because of their own sin, he points to Job's deepest vulnerability. Remember, Job had sacrificed regularly, "lest they curse God in their heart." Job regularly sacrificed for his children's thoughts to *avert* tragedy. At times, tragedy seems inexplicable. In our human striving to make sense out of the raw data of life, including its tragedies, some people today express thoughts similar to Bildad's.

In contrast to Eliphaz's experience of personal revelation, Bildad relies on tradition for his authority. Because Job suffers, Bildad assumes he is or may become one of the "godless." In a lengthy warning to Job, Bildad paints a portrait of someone who has forgotten God, whose hope dries up, and who withers "quicker than any grass." That person's "trust is a spider's web," he says—of no substance for support.

Bildad reassures Job further that if he will but seek God and if he is "blameless and upright," God will protect him and his home. There is still time to repent and to plead for God's mercy, he says. But we already know that Job is blameless and upright (1:1). Bildad also reassures Job of a brighter future: "Surely God does not reject a blameless man or strengthen the hands of evildoers. He will yet fill your mouth with laughter and your lips with shouts of joy. Your enemies will be clothed in shame, and the tents of the wicked will be no more" (8:19-22). His premature reassurance, however, fails to achieve its goal.

When Dr. David Scholer, former professor of the New Testament at the Fuller Theological Seminary, battled terminal cancer, people told him, "Don't worry; we all have to die," and "I know just how you feel."

He said, "Eventually, I came to overlook such remarks." Instead, such questions as "How are you dealing with your illness?" and "May I pray with you for strength for today?" would have helped him more.[5]

Distressed people need hope, but we show insensitivity when we, like Bildad, offer it misguidedly or prematurely. In the end, Job recovers and Bildad's promise of blessing comes true. However, right then, in depression, Job's mood makes it difficult for him to absorb almost any wisdom, advice, confrontation, or even hope. That's also true of people in tragedy today. If we were in Job's position, would Bildad's words have encouraged us? In recovery, timing is critical. In the healing process, patience to wait for the sufferer to be ready to hear what we have to say is as important as what we say.

Something Is Wrong

A long ramp leads to the entry of the home of the Rev. John Nelson. Pastor Nelson served churches in several western states for forty-one years. His son, Ron, after graduation from high school, worked at a Christian camp, taking campers to the lake for water sports. He dove off the boat ramp one day; unfortunately, the water was too shallow. When Ron struck his head, momentum snapped his neck.

The father recalls, "When Ron became a quadriplegic that changed life for everybody. With Ron, it wasn't just the break, but a series of surgeries and a lot of unknowns. It took a year for his physical recovery to progress to the point of greatest function."

"Then [came] the mental process of recovering from depression, grieving, not only because of the physical pain, but also because you've lost the son you had and you've got a new one; you've got to deal with that. We lost our future and have to take on a new future." Pastor Nelson's ability to acknowledge the loss of the son he once had and the recognition of a "new" son illustrates how well he coped with his changed life.

After the accident, church members mobilized for prayer. Some prayed diligently for Ron's healing. They led their children in prayer on their knees. Many kept checking, asking, "Is Ron better yet?" and "Is Ron walking yet?" "We're praying for him every day. God's going to heal him! We're going to have healing services for him," others said.

When Pastor Nelson wheeled him into church, however, one family responded: "We prayed for your son to be healed and God didn't heal him so there must be something wrong. Since he's the son of a pastor, there must be something wrong with the pastor, or God would have honored those prayers."

Because they didn't feel that they should raise their children in an environment where God was not honoring the pastor and church, they left the congregation. That group of church members believed God is honored only in a miraculous recovery from spinal cord injury. Similar to Beth who insisted on Jessica's confession of sin, they attributed something "wrong" to their pastor. God mercifully heals in many cases, but, as Joni Eareckson's and Ron's experiences demonstrate, those with spinal cord injury are not commonly among those whom God chooses to heal physically.

Innocent suffering baffles, frustrates, and creates so much pain for us that we are quick to offer explanations. When we sit with a sufferer, we rebel against our feeling of helplessness. We need to say something or feel compelled to blame someone. With no clear explanation evident, we may even blame the sufferer.

To his friends, Job is irreverent, impious, and dangerous: his vitriolic anger and bitterness against God reveal his sin. To Job, his friends are worse than useless, betrayers of his friendship, and hopelessly out of touch with his anguish. They fail even to acknowledge Job has cause to complain. Their defense of God blessing the righteous and punishing the wicked deafens them to Job's pain. That isolates them from compassionate understanding.

Learning to listen while accepting my helplessness enabled me as a young pastor to comfort many grieving widows in my first congregation. They frequently responded, "Thank you, pastor, I don't know what I would have done without you."

It Could Be Worse

> *For there are many sides to sagacity;*
> *And know that God has overlooked for you some of your*
> *iniquity (Zophar, Job 11:6).*

After Zophar listens carefully to Job's previous speeches, he attempts to turn Job's thoughts to a more hopeful perspective. But first he must deliver his reason for Job's tragedies. While Eliphaz represents those who trust personal revelation, and Bildad those who trust tradition, Zophar is our resident theologian. For him, God is so gracious that he spared Job the just deserts of his sin. Whereas Eliphaz offers only a general observation, "As I have seen, those who plow evil and sow mischief reap them," Zophar zeroes in on the culprit: "And know that God has overlooked for you some of your iniquity."

Throughout chapter 11, Zophar enumerates Job's other sins: disobedient pride (v. 13b), harboring secret sins (v. 14a), and injustice (v. 14b). He is most interested, however, in the hidden nature of divine wisdom, such that he can see Job's sins.[6] Zophar confronts

Job about his understanding of God's mysterious motives. Despite alluding to God's mercy in his indictment: 'God has overlooked for you some of your iniquity,' sadly, he offers Job no mercy.[7]

Zophar's response to Job's suffering warns any who seek the responsibility for counseling another. Because someone else has a problem at present, it's easy to forget that God also created that person in His image and likeness. The sufferer, therefore, usually has the strengths, capabilities, and gifts to enable him to work through his difficulties. Counseling is not a debate, argument, confrontation, or a contest of wills. We counsel to bring healing, not like Zophar to keep the upper hand.

Comforting others humbles us to walk with another in tragedy long enough to help them take the next step to help themselves. It may involve confronting reality, but only after patient listening and learning; only from a motive of compassion. We achieve this less through our words and more through our manner. We counsel best when we remain within the emotional limits of what the sufferer can tolerate. Counseling respects sufferers, regardless of their temporary difficulties.

The responses of Job's friends demonstrate the danger of jumping to conclusions. Because each of them feels a compulsion to convey what they understand, they cannot hear Job's anguish. It is vital, therefore, to focus on feelings at least as much as on information. It is also critical to check our assumptions about what the sufferer thinks or feels: ask them directly.

The attitudes of Job's friends, as we have seen, live on today. With Job we could well say, "Now you, too, have proved to be of no help" (Job 6:21). But do they also provide Job more help than he or they know?

Do Job's Friends Help?

If Job's three wisdom colleagues offer such cold comfort in their words, do they help him in any other way? Even though they fail Job in their inability to feel with him in his distress, they provide him with a major source of strength to sustain him through his crisis: social support.

As part of their support, these friends provide Job with a group experience where he can respond to each of them in turn. His friends, even in disagreement, provide him the utmost in respect.[8]

Eliphaz, Bildad, and Zophar respond to Job with an enormous demonstration of support. When they first hear of his tragedies, they meet, travel together, show their grief, and sit with him for a week until he feels ready to speak. Now, with their seemingly endless rounds of challenging Job with the teachings of wisdom, they also never leave Job. So eager are they to convince Job, they talk, argue, debate, confront, and counterattack chapter after chapter until Job (and the reader) feels worn out. But through it all, they stay. In fact, like his wife, the three friends stay until the end. How do you end your life if your friends never leave you alone? That's a clue to how we can help. As much as possible, we stay with the distressed person with regular follow-up contact: visits, phone calls, and cards.

CHAPTER 8

TIME OUT!

S INCE BEGINNING YOUR recovery, you've probably felt intense emotions. You may have felt desperate— even despaired—in the wake of tragedy. Or you may have asked the purpose of your life, fought through depression, anger, or fear. Your friends, you may have felt, didn't have a clue. Job also experienced those feelings. Because recovery demands hard work, we need time to gain perspective. Although easy to postpone or avoid, reflecting on the serious issues of life can pay big dividends. Melissa's reflection prepared her for what she least expected.

MELISSA REFLECTS

"I'm down from my ride," Melissa's husband Brad told her in his 7 a.m. call. "I'm on my way home." That morning he and his college roommate had ridden a hot-air balloon in a neighboring state. *It's good to know they're back down safely*, she thought. The drive home would take about three hours.

Melissa earlier feared for the safety of her son Daniel. Many times after curfew she lay in bed listening for the vroom of his Mustang. She wavered from: *Once he gets home, I'm going to clean his clock!* to *Please, Lord, let him come home safely.*

Then, she reflected: *Now Melissa, if a state trooper showed up in the middle of the night and said Dan hadn't made it, what would you really do?*

"I had just started preparing the food for a pot roast dinner for Brad and the kids," Melissa said of that mid-May Sunday afternoon. "I was sweaty from yard work with church teens that morning, so I interrupted my food preparation to shower. In my robe, with my hair in a towel, I looked out the upstairs window. When I saw a car with a state trooper parked outside, I thought, *That's really funny.*" After she dressed to answer the doorbell, however, she felt surprised to see her unexpected visitor.

"While driving home this morning," the state trooper said after being invited in, "your husband fell asleep at the wheel. He crossed the centerline and died on impact. I'm very sorry."

"I felt numb," Melissa said. "Life felt surreal. Then, as if on auto-pilot, I switched to survival mode: plan, sort, and think." *Okay, Who do I need to contact? What do I need to do first?* Melissa planned out the next hour. "After that," she said, "I knew I'd lose it." Forty-four, a widow with three children, Melissa began a new chapter in her life.

"I need you right now," Melissa phoned Dan, who had moved out of the home. Unaware of the trooper's visit, daughters Karen and Karla remained downstairs in the family room while Melissa called Jody, a church friend, to help console the girls. When Daniel and Jody arrived five minutes later, they walked downstairs together. After their "cry-fest," as Melissa called it, she called Brad's mother and her parents. "After that," she said, "my memory blurred."

Jody called the church elders. The youth leaders made sure Karen and Karla had friends to be with them. Another friend of

Melissa's arrived at the door, "casserole in one hand, sleeping bag in the other."

Melissa Reflects on Her Marriage

In addition to thinking through her response to potential family tragedy, Melissa had prepared herself in another way. To support her son's girlfriend through recovery from addiction, Melissa attended Christian twelve-step meetings with her. In those meetings, Melissa learned wisdom for times when life is out of control.

"I got more in touch with my feelings through the Celebrate Recovery program and the journaling. I learned to love my husband despite his issues. I realized that I needed to keep my side of the street clean and let him deal with his things—love him just the way he was. So I came to a peace within my marriage, with the little things. If I hadn't, I would have felt more guilt. Many times in our lives, God prepares us."

Through the support group, Melissa discovered wisdom to accept her inability to control her husband. After she learned to love him for himself, her ability to manage the tragedy of his death increased. Perhaps you face a frustrating situation or love a difficult person. Melissa's wisdom could help you. Step 1 begins, "We admitted we were powerless..." When we can admit our inability to control our tragic circumstances and other people (as well as our addictions), we've begun to recover.

Perhaps until now you've also found accepting your lack of control over events difficult. You may blame yourself or others or God. Instead of looking to change your circumstances or other people, you might adopt Melissa's wisdom: to love others for who they are. You may also need to learn to accept changed circumstances, however tragic.

Whereas Melissa discovered wisdom for tragedy before the event, Job reflects in the midst of recovery. In chapter 28, he takes time out from his self-defense to explore the nature of wisdom. The received wisdom of his friends fails to account for his experience. That experience defies even his own understanding of wisdom. He must search further for the reason for his suffering.

We all search for the reason for tragic events we experience, to make sense of our seemingly senseless circumstances. We need wisdom for weathering times of tragedy. Chapter 28 presents a serene mood of reflection.

Serene Reflection on Wisdom

> *There is a mine for silver, and a place where gold is refined.*
> *But where can wisdom be found; where is the place of*
> *understanding? (Job 28:1, 12).*

In this chapter, Job explores wisdom: precious but hidden. People search for it as they dig for stores of precious metals and gems, he says. Like gold and silver, we highly prize wisdom yet find it hidden, far from easy access. Although we dig deep to unearth copper and sapphires, where do we uncover wisdom?

> *God understands the way to it; He knows its place.*
> *Then He saw it and gauged it; He measured it and probed*
> *it (Job 28:23, 27).*

Earlier, because God had blocked Job's "way," life lost meaning. Now, Job concludes, only God knows the "way" to wisdom. As the all-seeing God viewed the earth He created, He saw, gauged, measured, and probed it. Now, if Job could only discover wisdom, personified as the primeval principle of creation,[1] the design of the universe, he could understand his painful losses.

In the final verse, we have God's answer.

> *[God] said to man, "See! Fear of the Lord is wisdom; to*
> *shun evil is understanding" (Job 28:28).*

That climactic statement as well as this whole reflective chapter leads Job away from his defensiveness, away from his pursuit of a lawsuit, to reflect on the source of wisdom for which he longs. Verse 28 carries particular significance for understanding the Book of Job. Like the two sides of a manila file folder, 28:28 and 1:1 (where Job from the beginning "fears the Lord" and "shuns evil") enclose the first half of the book. On the one hand, therefore, the answer in v. 28 appears to provide a formal closure to the book.[2] With this wisdom as fear (reverence, awe) of the Lord, Job returns to square one. However blameless and upright, however faithful in fearing God and shunning evil, Job still suffers tragedy. He still lacks sufficient wisdom to answer his question about unjust suffering: "Why?"

On the other hand, therefore, that verse as closure deceives.[3] In chapters 29–31, Job resumes his protest. That verse, therefore, does not end the book. With Job, we're left with the inadequacy of the traditional wisdom answer. Job will no longer seek wisdom through personal devotion but will pursue—even intensify—his demand for direct personal access to God to clear his name.

REFLECTION ON RECOVERY—JOB'S AND OURS

How does Job recover? Three important factors stand out: the social support of his friends, his honest expression of his true feelings, and his refusal to remain a victim. Related to all of these is a fourth factor: his relationship with God. Although his friends misunderstand Job, they also keep Job focused on Him. We have seen Job's willingness to risk blasphemy to express his true emotions. At first worshipful and trusting, he later rages at God for his life of meaningless suffering. When his friends fail to understand him, he pursues God to sue for justice.

Job models a way to voice a healthy dispute with God over tragedy. Like many people today, you may feel embarrassed or ashamed for your complaints against Him. Job, however, presents a way to confront God honestly with complete freedom, to express to Him our true feelings. With such a step, you could feel liberated, knowing He welcomes you as you are.

As you reflect on your recovery, what factors do you see at work? Maybe you can identify family, neighbors, or church friends as sources of social support similar to Job's or to Melissa's. Maybe you've not found the answer, but you've learned to say how you feel. True, it hasn't "solved" your loss, but it may have helped you feel relieved. Maybe you've taken steps to move away from the role of victim and begun to take responsibility for how you respond. You've undertaken a plan to cope with your loss in a way that gives you control. Maybe your recovery has taken a very different turn from what I suggest here, but you may find, as did Job and Melissa, that there is value in taking time out to reflect, to discover wisdom for when your life is out of control.

To wisdom for recovery drawn from Job and from people today, we can add wisdom drawn from an important figure from the past. Except for a college course in the classics, you may never have heard his name. Yet his life and his writings provide us with a treasure trove of wisdom, as it did for people experiencing tragedy who have read his work for centuries after he lived.

Recovery in Historical Perspective: Boethius

Disaster, tragedy, destruction, and death are not new issues. Nor are ways for people to find hope for recovery. During the Middle Ages, for example, people reflected on suffering brought about by constant wars, enslavement, and the bubonic plague. They developed a paradigm of a universal and continuous cycle on which they plotted success, disaster, deprivation, and recovery on a wheel, the Wheel of Life.

Although he didn't originate it, the Roman philosopher

Anicius Manlius Severinus Boethius (d. 524 AD), through his exposition of the Wheel of Life in *The Consolation of Philosophy,* enabled millions of people to find hope for their recovery. Writing from personal experience, Boethius illustrates the slippery nature of success, the cyclical nature of recovery, and the need for a deeper relationship with God.

Boethius's leadership qualities attracted the attention of the Ostrogoth leader Theodoric, king of Rome and the western half of the Roman Empire.[4] After Boethius performed important assignments for him in 510 AD, Theodoric appointed him Consul without Companion, one of the most prestigious of all Roman positions. Although honorary, many Roman men envied him that title. It afforded him the honor of presiding over the games, which made him popular in Rome. Later Theodoric promoted him to *magister officiorum,* which led to leadership of the civil service and to oversight of palace officials. In 522 Theodoric also appointed Boethius's two sons Consuls Together, a notable recognition of the confidence in their father, both by Theodoric in Rome and by the Christian emperor in Constantinople.

In a dispute over theology with political ramifications, Boethius sided with Constantinople—and for Christian unity. That, however, threatened Theodoric's position: people saw Theodoric as a heretic and an invading Ostrogoth barbarian. Boethius's opponents produced evidence, some say spurious, to implicate him in the election of the pro-Constantinople Pope John I. Theodoric ordered Boethius arrested, sentenced, and exiled to await execution. Intimidated, the Roman Senate confirmed his sentence. After brutal beating and torture, a year after his arrest, Boethius died at Pavia, Italy, in exile.[5]

The Consolation of Philosophy

As the once honored Boethius awaits execution, however, he reflects—and writes. In *The Consolation of Philosophy,* he pictures Philosophy as a woman from whom, in his cell, he seeks consolation as he reflects on the classic problem of evil.

> But the greatest cause of my sadness is really this – the fact that in spite of a good helmsman to guide the world, evil can still exist and even pass unpunished. This fact alone you must surely think of considerable wonder. But there is something even more bewildering. When wickedness rules and flourishes, not only does virtue go unrewarded, it is even trodden under foot by the wicked and punished in place of crime. That this can happen in the realm of an omniscient and omnipotent God who wills only good is beyond perplexity and complaint. (Book IV, 1)

Boethius defines the issue with which Job struggles and with which we also struggle: How does an all-knowing, all-powerful, and good God permit evil to go unpunished and virtue unrewarded? Like Job, Boethius says he had done everything right: how could God allow him to suffer unjustly?

This thought may well trouble you as you also struggle with your undeserved suffering. You try to figure out how, when you've done your utmost to do right, you still suffer. No matter how you figure it, you come up blank. You may have little idea how your own actions caused or contributed to your present dire circumstances.

Boethius warns us of the short-lived nature of success. No one was more aware of the fickleness of success than he. In the poetry of the first part of his book, he describes his own rise— and sudden fall.

> First fickle Fortune gave me wealth short-lived,
> Then in a moment all but ruined me.
> Since Fortune changed her trustless countenance,
> Small welcome to the days prolonging life.
> Foolish the friends who called me happy then
> Whose fall shows how my foothold was unsure. (I, 1)

Despite the uncertainty of life, Boethius provides hope for those who, like him, find ourselves distressed, depressed, and lost, and who struggle toward recovery. If life is uncertain, and success fleeting, how do we recover? Philosophy depicts life's uncertainty as a person poised on the rim of a wheel. Life's circular and impermanent nature offered Boethius a perspective on suffering. See Fortune Turning the Wheel of Life.[6]

With Fortune at the right turning the wheel, we note how at the top, in regal garments, crown, and scepter, we reign as king (and queen). As Fortune moves the wheel, however, we lose our crown. Head first we tumble, off balance. Time marches on so that, like Job, by the time we find ourselves at the bottom, we've not only lost our crown but our fall has emptied our pockets of money. Impoverished, destitute, and hopeless, our life has turned upside down—and so have we. We hold on for dear life. As Time continues, however, so does our fortune: clad in fancy shoes and a new hat, we grab a spot on the Wheel of Life to lift us. Clothed again, we can even look up. Eventually, we again approach the top.

To avoid the wide (and more devastating) swings of life, Philosophy counsels Boethius to move toward the Center, i.e., toward God.

> Whatever moves any distance from the primary intelligence becomes enmeshed in ever-stronger chains of Fate, and everything is the Freer from Fate the closer it seeks the center of things. And if it cleaves to the steadfast mind of God, it is free from movement and so escapes the necessity imposed by Fate. (IV, 6)

Although God is conceived here more in terms of the God of the philosophy of the time, the experience of believers validates Boethius's wise advice: the closer we draw to God, the less we feel the effects of the changing circumstances of life, its ups and downs— especially its downs.[7] In the midst of tragedy, says Boethius, draw close to God.

MELISSA'S RECOVERY

Even as our success sours, so also do we usually recover from our worst misfortune. The Wheel of Life continues its rotation. That can give us perspective on how to get through our present tragic circumstances and give us hope for our recovery. Two main sources of support enabled Melissa to overcome her tragedy.

People made a big difference. After friends "traipsed through my front door, hug after hug, I also recognized I needed to express gratitude. Out of kindness, people I didn't know provided dinners for two months, took out the garbage, picked up my mail, and cleaned my gutters." Through all her sorrow, she allowed her thankfulness to flow, too. "I wouldn't have felt gratitude so strongly without my tragic loss," she said.

Although friends proved helpful, Melissa found her greatest support, as Boethius counseled, in God. "I realized I couldn't survive on my own," Melissa said. "Because my emotions felt so raw, I drove myself to seek God. At first I talked with God every hour. I acknowledged my lack of control and asked God for help." That awareness of God's presence got her through. "I felt grateful that I enjoyed that kind of relationship with God," she said. That relationship provided a specific perspective from which to view her tragedy.

"People asked, 'Why would this happen?' and 'Why would God do this?'" *God doesn't waste a hurt,* she thought. "I realized I had an understanding and a peace through the tragedy. I didn't understand the reason Brad died, just that there was one. I realized later that, unaware, I had set an example for others in understanding life and death." By giving her peace through tragedy, God worked through her to help others.

After security, disaster, and sadness comes the long road to recovery. We measure progress in tiny, almost-imperceptible increments. Melissa called on God for help hour-by-hour. She also identified a clear set of steps that helped her begin her long road to recovery.

"First," Melissa said, "I recognized that I needed to walk through the pain. I made a commitment to myself that I wouldn't use an external escape such as wine."

"Second, I told my children that as a family, we were like a table with only three legs." She then asked, "How will we reposition those legs to make them all a table again? We need to work together, pray together, and care for each other in a whole new way."

"Third, I began to journal." As she later reread her journal entries, "I discovered how much my faith had countered others' doubts."

"Fourth, prayer helped overcome helplessness. For the first time in my life, I realized I had no control. For the first time in my walk with God, I let Him take 100 percent control. That's something I continue to practice.

"Finally, I needed to become a part of the church in a new way. I wanted to be able to help other people the same way they helped me," she said. As part of helping others, she joined a series of twelve-step programs, including leading one in her own church.

Melissa's (and Our) Circle of Life

Melissa's story of tragedy fits the pattern noted centuries ago. At first, we begin with the wind at our back. Everything goes well; we are on top of the world. Job ascends to become the greatest man in the East. Boethius takes charge of the king's palace. Melissa, wife, mother of three, looks forward to Sunday afternoon dinner with husband and children.

Then, usually without warning, disaster strikes. We lose big time. A quick succession of four messengers reports to Job disaster after disaster—climaxing in the death of his children. Political enemies accuse Boethius of treason. A state trooper rings Melissa's doorbell.

However, despite our deepest losses and severest depressions, we slowly adjust to our new condition, to survival strategies, and begin to recover. Job finds support in his friends, expresses his most frightening thoughts, and begins to petition God. Boethius, though sentenced to death, writes what will become a book of hope for millions over the next thousand years. Melissa, grateful, seeks ways to serve others. Eventually, as the wheel continues to turn, we may return to a position stronger than we thought possible.

How to
Obtain Wisdom

If you seek to increase your wisdom, take time to reflect on these issues and jot your thoughts in your journal:

1. **The frailty of life.** Scripture describes our life as grass (Psalm 103:15-16; 1 Peter 1:24, quoting Isaiah 40:6-8), and as a vanishing mist (James 4:14). Reflect on your vulnerability to reverses, some of them potentially tragic. Although we anticipate no disaster, we also enjoy no guarantee of our prosperity, safety, or comfort. What would *you* do in a sudden, severe, reversal?

2. **God the center.** Where does God or a Higher Power fit in with your philosophy? If you reject the idea of a personal God, as presented in the Book of Job, what have you substituted for your center? If you embrace a personal God, where do you place Him? At the periphery of your life? At your center? Where do *you* find stability through the fluctuating fortunes of life?

3. **The source of hope.** Where do you find hope? What gives you the ability to overcome the tragedies you've faced? How have family, friends, other believers, prayer, circumstances, and/or Scripture helped *you* in your darkest hour?

4. **The reality of evil.** How would you answer the questions Boethius and Melissa's friends asked about the presence of evil in a world created by a good God?

CHAPTER 9

OH, THE GOOD OLE DAYS

AFTER A LOVED-ONE's death, I often ask parishioners, "What do you miss most?" Their faces flush, tears appear, then flow. My question usually generates a detailed description of one or two of the loved one's most cherished qualities. Those memories reawaken grief but also bring relief. The bereaved can share their most cherished memories, enabling them to remember, share, and integrate more memories of the lost loved one. Their intensified grief seems to help them move on.

SURPRISED BY GRIEF

By the time doctors correctly diagnosed Laurie's bladder cancer, it had grown to Stage IV and infected her lymph nodes. After surgery, longer and more extensive than expected, the doctors told her husband Hank "the probabilities for her survival."

"Until then," he said, "it hadn't occurred to me that I would outlive Laurie. I had pictured us together the rest of our lives, with me the first to die." *Like most men,*

I won't need to grieve, Hank thought. That dawning reality of Laurie's death, however, was catastrophic for him. He says,

> After Laurie's three years of chemotherapy, radiation, another false all-clear, and a second surgery that left her with a colostomy as well as a urostomy, she began to hallucinate and to deny necessary medical treatment. One month shy of our twenty-fourth wedding anniversary, Laurie died.
>
> I miss most about Laurie the "grace-full" quality of our relationship. As a Christian, I believed in the theology of grace: God freely blesses us, unworthy sinners, not because of our achievements or goodness, but on the basis of his love. I was as orthodox as anybody. But Laurie gave me an emotional grasp of the doctrine of grace: having been given a gift so great, so undeserved, I looked for ways to reciprocate. I didn't feel like I was paying back or earning. That was a whole new experience for me.

As he looks back, Hank misses the love Laurie gave so freely.

As you look back on some important person you've lost, what do you miss most? Maybe you miss their sweet smile or tender touch, their generous spirit, their passionate zest for living, or their indomitable courage. What you miss most is characteristic of your friend or loved one and of your relationship.

When Job looks back, he also recalls what he misses most.

> *Job again took up his theme and said: O that I were in the months gone by, in the days when God watched over me (Job 29:1-2).*

Before a group of friends and elders assembled as judge and jury, in chapters 29–31 Job delivers his closing arguments. That audience also includes God. Once and for all, he aims to provoke God to confront him—face to face—with the charges against him. As if to shout "Answer me!" Job again defends his innocence. He takes up his legal testimony,[1] looks back on his losses, and pinpoints what he misses most. For the first time also, we feel his sadness.

REMEMBER, REMEMBER HARD, TURN AWAY

To remember what we miss most represents an important step in our grieving. In grief, we work to resolve the tension between our life before our loss and our life after. Though emotionally painful, remembering helps us grieve.

Job Remembers

> *O that I were in the months gone by, in the days when God watched over me,*
> > *When his lamp shone over my head, when I walked in the dark by its light,*
> > *When I was in my prime, when God's company graced my tent, when Shaddai was still with me (Job 29:2-5).*

Of all he loses: family, businesses, employees, wealth, and health, Job mentions first God's presence. Job knows God, reveres God, and worships God. As a righteous patriarch, he sacrifices to the Lord on behalf of his children. Even after catastrophe, he worships and praises the Lord. With his wife, he comes to God's defense, even to accept the presence of evil from God.

Throughout his arguments with his colleagues, Job expresses depression, anger, and fear—but not sadness. Even during his deepest depression, Job doesn't express the sadness of his losses. As we try to repair the damage done by circumstances, we can also withdraw into depression so that we shut down nearly everything, such as awareness of our true emotions and our important relationships.

Now, feeling deep sadness, Job remembers how it was for him not so long before, when God watched over him. Given his previous image of God as a hostile Watcher, that statement surprises us. Each of Job's comments reflects his loss. God had watched over him but now He spies. God had once protected him but now viciously attacks. God had been a friend who shared his tent but now remains silent.[2] As his memories flood, Job longs for earlier days.

We also remember how it was for us. Life wasn't perfect then, but it was a lot better than it is now. Now that we've lost so much, what wouldn't we give to have it back, and, perhaps, with it, the sense of God's presence? God's company might again grace our tent, our home. Whether we've lost our spouse, our child, our health, our business, our possessions, our money, our retirement, or our dearest friend, when we remember, it hurts.

In missing the sense of God's presence, even prayer can feel meaningless. That's how it was for me during many years of our children's downhill spiral. *What good does it do to pray? Nothing happens. In fact, "change" seems always to mean "for the worse."* However, despite no effective prayer, no sense of communion with the Lord, no meaningful connection with the Word, and despite my feelings, during those years I stayed close to our local congregation and to our small fellowship group. Eventually meeting with, talking, and praying with Christian friends, I felt my sense of God's presence slowly return.

When my lads surrounded me (Job 29:5).

Job identifies not only the loss he misses most, but other losses as well. He misses his "lads." Most translations say "sons," but the same word is used in chapter 1 for "servants." God was Job's first priority, but the symbols of God's blessing were his servants. With the death of his lads, he loses his role as leader, patriarch, and business mogul. As he recalls those who looked up to him and who depended on him, he expresses sadness and wistful longing. For Job, as for many of us, material blessing evidences God's presence.

When my feet were bathed in cream and rocks poured out
streams of oil for me (Job 29:6).

Job misses the "good old days," especially the material pro-
vision of luxury. As the Lord enabled Moses to obtain water
from a rock in the wilderness at Horeb and sustained his people
through honey and cream from the rocks in the Promised Land,[3]
so Job remembers his former life as one of pampered treatment.

Do you remember when you last bathed your feet in cream? I
don't either. Here Job remembers a past far more luxurious that
it was in reality. In other words, he idealizes his lost past. We
do that, too. When we lose a spouse, our marriage was the best!
We ignore all the struggles, conflicts, and hurts. When we lose
our job, we remember the great company parties, camaraderie
with coworkers, the bosses' praise and our paycheck. We forget
the long hours, the ridicule of one colleague, or our supervisor's
crushing annual review of performance. Do you catch yourself
latching on to certain unrealistic glorified images of your past? If
you could recall the more difficult memories with your lost loved
one along with those you cherish, you might shorten the grieving
process. Would you then feel more guilt? To come to terms with
the weaknesses of lost loved ones as well as their strengths will
help forge a realistic view of their lives—and ours.

When I passed through the city gates to take my seat in the
square,
    Young men saw me and hid, elders rose and stood...
    For I saved the poor man who cried out, the orphan who
had none to help him (Job 29:7, 12).

Job also misses justice, justice he administered. He reminds his
jury how, as an ideal elder, he saved the poor, the orphan, the
wretched, the widow, and the stranger. He judged justly at the
city gate. As he builds up his own ideal image of justice, God's

justice suffers by comparison.[4] From the standpoint both of a legal defense and of emotional grief, he recalls that loss of justice.

> *I thought I would end my days with my family (literally 'nest') (Job 29:18).*

Like Hank, who thought Laurie would outlive him, Job recalls his lost dream, to end his days in his "nest." I know the bitterness of having my dreams dashed. Five years younger than I, my attractive sister Nancy began in her teen years to use alcohol to excess. I dreamed of the day when Nancy and I would draw closer. On a Sunday afternoon, however, as I arrived home from leading worship, I struggled to turn the key fast enough to grab the ringing phone.

"She's gone, Gordon, she's gone," Mom sobbed, from across the continent. At age 38, Nancy had died the previous night of internal hemorrhaging, the result of decades of alcohol abuse and lack of self-care. None of us expects to bury our brother, sister, or child. Beyond losing my sister, I lost my unrealistic dream of a closer relationship with her. During the visiting hours, funeral, burial, and days, weeks, and months following, I thought the intense emotional pain would never end. The death of my dream intensified the normal pain of my grief.

> *My words were as drops of dew upon them . . .*
> *When I smiled at them they would never believe it; they never expected a sign of my favor (Job 29:22, 24).*

To those in disputes at the city gate, Job dispenses more than justice. He remembers his words of refreshment and his smile akin to that of God's grace. In his gracious treatment of the persons involved, Job recalls his godly, even God-like demeanor.[5] Like God, he loved those whom he judged.

> *I decided their course and presided over them;*

> *I lived like a king among his troops, like one who con-*
> *soles mourners (Job 29:25).*

As a respected elder, Job remembers his power. A decision-maker for disputants, he presided at the city gate to hear their complaints and to resolve their conflicts. His image strikes us as highly narcissistic: not a king merely among *his people* but among *his troops.*[5] He recalls having exercised life-and-death power.

As he remembers his material blessings, Job accuses God of injustice. Not only are his lads gone, but also honor: elders, nobles, princes, the people, the needy, the blind, the lame, and the stranger all honored him. Job crushed evildoers, graciously blessed those whom he judged, and benevolently decided for others. All those blessings signaled God's presence. Everything that once gave his life meaning Job now remembers. In your grief, what do you remember?

Remember Hard

Another step in normal grief is to remember hard.

> *But now those younger than I deride me, [men] whose*
> *father I would have disdained to put among my sheep dogs*
> *(Job 30:1).*

"But now," says Job. What a contrast between the good old days and now! From a time of power, prominence, and position, the younger generation now ridicules him. That social reversal brings him the misery of shame. In chapter 30, as he continues his summary defense, now in terms of his present shame, his memories intensify his grief. When we remember our losses, we grieve. Instead of letting up, however, our grief may intensify.

Shame involves some objective act that breaks with the expectations of a group and that results in an internal sense of condemnation.[7] In Job's case, younger people now despise him for his condition. He devotes eighteen verses to detailing the many ways he experiences the humiliation of people from whom he should command respect. As he struggles to cover the wound to his self-respect, he feels humiliated.

"Now I am the butt of their jibes; I have become a byword to them... They do not withhold their spittle from my face" (vv. 9–10). His humiliation and disgrace from people who are far beneath him socially intensifies his grief. In his awareness of his frailty, Job also feels that shame before God: "[God] regarded me as clay. I have become like dust and ashes" (v. 19).

Job's exposed physical weakness before God further intensifies his shame in the form of feeling worthless.

> *I cry out to You, but You do not answer me; I wait, but You do not consider me.*
>
> *You have become cruel to me; with Your powerful hand you harass me.*
>
> *You lift me up and mount me on the wind; You make my courage melt (Job 30:20-22).*

As he had earlier, Job addresses God. Now the recollection of God's silence intensifies his grief: Job feels God responds with cruelty, sadism, and deceit. After He lifts Job up in honor, He drops him from his grand position. Job's courage evaporates.

> *I know You will bring me to death, the house assigned for all the living (Job 30:23).*

Job expects to die in abject misery. With God's abandonment, he will die in spiritual crisis, as well.

Periodically, Job reflects on his own death. How realistic are we about our death, "the house assigned for all living?" How often do we reflect on our own death? We customarily avoid thinking, talking, and planning it. But we miss an important opportunity:

learning to die well. "Isn't that why we're all working so hard?" the hospice nurse in my neighborhood asked me. "To die well?"

When we care for the dying said Elizabeth Kübler-Ross, they give us a special gift—the ability to accept our own death.

> *Did I not weep for the unfortunate? Did I not grieve for the needy?*
>
> *I looked forward to good fortune, but evil came...My bowels are in turmoil without respite...I walk about in sunless gloom; I rise in the assembly and cry out (Job 30:24-28).*

Despite Job weeping for the unfortunate and, as a result, expecting good fortune for himself, evil comes; his guts churn; he walks in perpetual shadows. When he rises in the assembly to cry out for justice, his community, like God, ignores his plea. "I have become a brother to jackals," he says in v. 29, "a companion to ostriches." Job's social isolation results from his blackened, peeling skin and charred bones (v. 30).

Job's shame overwhelms him. His peers, those on whose behalf he administered justice, and God, all reject him. He has breached the norms of his group, and, as a result, he feels condemned, exposed, and worthless. Nothing is left for Job but to mourn his death.

"So my lyre is given over to mourning, my pipe to accompany weepers," he concludes (v. 31).

Like Job, Hank recalls hard memories of Laurie's death. Her image flashes before him.

> I had never been with a dying person. I found the sights and sounds hard to bear. I had to deal with startlingly vivid flashbacks of Laurie's resistance to going to the hospital, and to her gasping for breath as her body slowed down in the dying process. I heard sounds that recalled those times, and fear surged through me. That left me exhausted and in a state of heightened wariness long after.

I remembered the doctor's assessment of Josh Lyman's trauma on a "West Wing" TV episode. Lyman had witnessed a shooting in Maryland. "You have to be able to remember that time without reliving it," the doctor said. "You're reliving it."

That hasn't happened to me for over a month and I really believe it's mostly over.

So many things seemed very sad to me. When I came back to the house, I found a clamp on a stick that Laurie used to take preserves off the top shelf of our pantry. I dissolved into tears. There wasn't anyone living in the house anymore who would ever need that stick.[8]

Reminded of his loss, Hank remembers hard. We remember hard at times involuntarily, as some action or event triggers our intensified grief. Although painful, the intensified grief foreshadows a turning toward our new life. To pinpoint that one special quality helps identify what the living want most to carry with them into their new life.

Turn Away

I have covenanted with my eyes not to gaze on a maiden.
   Calamity is surely for the iniquitous; misfortune for the worker of mischief.
   Surely he observes my ways, takes account of my every step (Job 31:1, 3–4).

Only after Job remembers, then remembers hard, does he, in chapter 31, turn away. Job returns to his ongoing lawsuit. Although he maintains his lost closeness with God as his first priority, his own innocence runs a close second. Because God had so far chosen to remain silent about His charges against him, in chapter 31 Job swears in detail his innocence of any wrongdoing. He then issues a *climactic legal challenge.*

Job defends himself: he consciously avoids the most common male temptation—lust. He invokes an oath of retribution should he act on improper sexual impulse. Further, he admits of no negligence of the needs of his servants ("man or maid"), the poor, the widow, or the orphan. He does not trust in money. He harbors no secret idolatry toward heavenly bodies. He does not rejoice over his enemy's downfall, nor, to bring about his enemy's death, does he curse him. He provides hospitality to the stranger. He has consciously avoided all sins.

"Where is my fault?" Job cries out. As he turns away from the intensity of his loss to refocus on his innocence, Job issues one last desperate challenge.

> *O that I had someone to give me a hearing;*
> *O that Shaddai would reply to my writ,*
> *Or my accuser draw up a true bill! I would carry it on*
> *my shoulder;*
> *Tie it around me for a wreath. I would give Him an*
> *account of my steps,*
> *Offer it as to a commander (Job 31:35–37).*

Job's challenge in chapter 31 takes the form of a "writ," a legal document that will, he hopes, force God to confirm or deny. It requires a response. On the one hand, if God remains silent, Job's innocence stands. That would put God in the wrong for having punished Job unjustly. On the other hand, if Job is guilty, he can expect a quick end to his misery.

To conclude his suit, Job desires two very specific helps: an impartial arbiter to judge and a legal document of charges (a "true bill") drawn by his accuser. If God delivers such a bill, Job will publicly display it. He will wear God's false charges with pride as a victory crown for all to see. He gives account and fully anticipates exoneration. He has now moved on from his grief back to the issue that dogged him all along—his innocence. He has done everything to provoke the Sovereign Creator of the universe to respond to his cry. God has yet to respond. We smile at Job's audacity to sue God. We can, however, learn some important lessons from his example.

Through Job's eyes we see our own petty reflection of how we wish life were. I wish my son and daughter-in-law had not gotten sick, and my sister hadn't died. Because reality at times can be brutal, we tend to deny the possibility of tragedy beforehand, and use wishful thinking after. Given what happened, my wishes, like Job's, appear unrealistic.

Job's pursuit of a lawsuit, though futile, demonstrates his inner mental strength. In his suffering unjustly, Job uses well the only framework available to him to pursue justice: take it to the King. *The more he litigates, the less he talks of death.* While he uses the option of lawsuit and the social support of his friends, Job keeps himself alive long enough to hear God speak. In the process of pursuing God in court, he gets better.

When we suffer wrongly, that is our recourse, too. Like those who suffer death for Jesus in Revelation 6:10 and take their case to the Sovereign Lord, we have a King who cares. Like Job when we demand an answer, we don't always hear back how or when we want. Nevertheless, God answers in His sovereign time and way.

There's another positive side to Job's lawsuit. Integral to his ranting about God's harassment is his belief in God's justice. He believes that, if he can only provoke God to respond, God will be fair. We can be sure of that, too.

Moving On

In his letter to family and friends quoted earlier, Hank describes how much he and Laurie particularly enjoyed Sir Neville Marriner's Academy of St. Martin in the Fields recording of Mozart's Symphony No. 35. Named for the man who commissioned it, they shared a special name for that particular recording, "our Haffner." Listening to it caused them to laugh out loud together.

"It's a virtual pun in four movements," Hank said. "However," he continued, "our copy acquired more scratches than Turtle Wax could cover, and the fourth movement was entirely gone." When Hank tried to buy another copy, he discovered that particular recording was no longer available. He, therefore, substituted a recording of the same symphony, with the same orchestra, but by another director.

"It wasn't the same," he said. "It was good but not in the ways the old one was. I probably liked the old one so much because we knew it so well and liked it together. I caught myself pushing the new one away because it wasn't as good as the old one. But I saw the power of the analogy and something inside me relaxed. My whole body relaxed." With that recognition, he had turned away and moved on.

"I had to hear new music and not judge it by its fidelity to the old standard," Hank said, "but simply by whether it spoke to me now. It wasn't a translation of a past, but a clean shot at a future."

What Helped Hank Most

"My initial grief response was emotional," Hank said, "but I received little satisfaction or release from direct expression of my emotions. When I read *Men Don't Cry... Women Do,* however, I found more help another way."

In that book, the authors observe that the emotional grief response is *intuitive.* Some people experience grief as feelings, people who "reveal vivid brief glimpses of intense inner pain, helplessness, hopelessness, and loneliness."[9] Generally, but not exclusively, women tend to express their grief that way. But for Hank, "feelings are fuel that helps me get someplace else. They're not a pool that I get in and splash around in. It's like people who are in the intuitive mode get in a swimming pool. They splash around and then they feel so much better."

"I responded better to what the authors call the *instrumental pattern*," said Hank. These people, men generally, think more, tone down their feelings, and desire to master them. At the same time, they talk less about those feelings but engage more in problem solving. "Blended grievers" combine traits of both styles.

"I realized I'd been trying to jam myself into an intuitive style," Hank said, "when I am an instrumental type. I'm an instrumental everything, which means I'm an instrumental griever. I thought things out and developed a vocabulary, concepts, and expectations." Hank tells of a conversation with his brother Andy.

"Have you considered anti-depressants?" Andy asked.

"No, it never occurred to me," Hank said.

"Well, aren't you depressed?"

"Yeah, I am, but I'm not any more depressed than I ought to be."

Reflecting on that conversation, Hank says, "I developed a plausible line of decline into and recovery from grief. I was right on the line, so I wasn't nervous or anxious about it. I felt bad, but I wasn't feeling any worse than I should have been feeling. I expected to feel better in due time. To know that I wasn't feeling worse than I should have helped me."

Another strategy we've seen in Job and others also helped Hank—social support. "I was with people who knew me and knew Laurie. I went to movies with them; I went to dinners with them; I went to concerts with them. I actively sought more social contacts than ever before in my life—but not new contacts. I wasn't interested in making new friends, because that was too hard. However, I saw somebody every day, rigorously. And on the weekends, two of the three weekend nights I was with somebody, doing something."

Hank also contacted a counselor who specialized in grief. She shared new ideas to help him further resolve his grief, but Hank's instrumental strategies helped him most turn away from his grief and move on with life.[10]

How to
Live With Grief

1. Anticipate mood shifts from normalcy to sadness and back. Almost anything or anyone can trigger an emotional response during a period of grieving. Keeping a journal can help you identify fluctuating feelings.

2. Find people to share your memories, such as friends, clergy, and church members. Encourage them to call or contact you. Otherwise they may assume that you prefer to be alone. Let them know what you need.

3. Identify, if possible, your particular style of grieving: intuitive, instrumental, or blended. Determine to do those activities or to be with people who would help you most.

4. Read Scriptures of comfort, consolation, and hope, such as the Psalms.

5. Read books on how others have dealt with grief. Explore communities of grievers on the Internet.

How to
Move On

1. After you recognize your need to grieve, recognize also your need to resolve your grief and to move on with your life. Recording your thoughts, feelings, and experiences in your journal can enable you to grieve and to move on.

2. Identify, if possible, where you are in your process of grieving: remembering, remembering hard, or moving on. If you find it hard to move on, you may have attempted to do so without allowing yourself to fully grieve. You may need to consult your doctor or a counselor to help free you. Likewise if you find it difficult to remember, you may be traumatized by your loss and require professional help.

3. Ignore the shame-based: "You should be over this by now," whether from others or from yourself. Every person grieves at his or her own pace. If guilt or shame after a death persists longer than three months, however, consider professional help from your doctor, pastor, or a counselor.

4. Take opportunities to spend time with people who knew your loved one. They will welcome the opportunity to support you.

5. Depending on your individual circumstances, begin to plan new activities, accept family responsibilities, and adopt new projects meaningful to you.

6. Read Scriptures on hope, encouragement, on victory over death and over the fear of death, such as Psalms, Hebrews and Revelation.

7. Read self-help books on overcoming grief.

PART THREE

A MODEL OF TRANSFORMATION

FROM RECOVERY TO TRANSFORMATION

CHAPTER 10

SEEKING COMMON GROUND

Y OU'VE LEARNED TO cope with your tragedy. What at first seemed an unmitigated disaster turns out to have some good outcomes: memories you cherish, friends who support you, professionals who provide a trusting relationship or groups to which you belong that rally to your side. At first, survival seemed a distant dream, but slowly you've made significant, hard-won progress. You're more at peace. Even your feeling that God abandoned you may have begun to fade. With what happened to you, you needed to talk, to find others who would hear your story. Now you may have the opposite need—to listen.

"Pastor, could I talk with you?" Beverly asked in a phone call. With her husband and family she engaged as an active, faithful parishioner. Beverly agreed to meet in Pastor Steve's office. *She sounds distressed*, he thought, *she's never sought my counsel before.* In his big overstuffed counseling chair, Beverly explained the reason for her visit.

"Every morning," she said, "I'm embarrassed to admit I have to slip across the street in my bathrobe, camping on my girlfriend's doorstep, I call it. With Jason's wedding coming up, I can't do anything else. It helps me get through the day to talk with Martha. I know I can't stay like this," she said, "but I don't know what else to do."

I'm not sure how to help, either, Pastor Steve thought as Beverly talked. *She seems immobilized, probably needs more than what I can provide.* "Let me take you to where you can talk with someone who can evaluate you," Pastor Steve said.

"I'll go," said Beverly. She called home to let her husband know.

Pastor Steve drove Beverly to the local psychiatric hospital for evaluation. After the assessment, the chief psychiatrist invited Steve to the staff discussion of her case.

"How is Beverly's relationship with God?" the chief psychiatrist asked Steve during the staff meeting.

"Poor," he replied.

"Notice how her depression is cutting her off from God as well as from other people," the psychiatrist said.

The doctor was right. When we feel depressed, God, as well as other people, seems far away. After Beverly's evaluation, the hospital prescribed anti-depressant medication and referred her to a psychiatrist in private practice for ongoing therapy. That treatment, along with continued visits with Pastor Steve, helped bring Beverly out of depression.

Beverly had lost all joy in life. Her depressed mood, like Job's, represented a significant change from her normal functioning, a clue she needed professional help.

But Beverly's story reveals another aspect of depression identified by the hospital staff. As Beverly updated her pastor, she described her evaluation experience. In the middle of the session, the nurse brought her up short by saying, "You haven't heard a word I've said." Beverly quoted the nurse to Pastor Steve and told him how that confrontation had stunned her. "I realized that she was right. I wasn't listening to her at all!" Only after the nurse confronted her did Beverly realize that she felt so intent on conveying her distress, she had shut out everyone else. Like Beverly, in your distress from tragedy, unintentionally perhaps you also have shut others out.

Because of your loss, especially if it is a tragic loss, you want everyone to know how much you hurt. It's been painful to patiently listen to other people's concerns or others' interaction with you, let alone welcome their suggestions or advice. In depression we cut ourselves off from God and from other people. Like Job with God and with his friends, we can focus on our own anguish to such an extent that we find listening to others difficult. Without minimizing our distress, however, there comes a time to acknowledge others' contributions to our recovery. As with Beverly, Job also experiences an unexpected confrontation.

JOB'S "IMPARTIAL" ARBITER

Then Elihu...was angry—angry with Job because he thought himself right against God (Job 32:2).[1]

Chapters 32–37 contain a brief personal introduction to Elihu, followed by a lengthy series of his speeches. In these discourses, Elihu gives his reasons for speaking up (32), outlines his case against Job (33), twice defends God's justice (34, 36-37), and explains the reasons why God remains distant from people (35). In response to Job's lawsuit with God, Elihu appoints himself mediator. He thus fulfills Job's longing expressed in chapter 9: "No arbiter is between us to lay his hand on us both."

Elihu plays a paradoxical role. He claims to want to vindicate Job, but in the end defends God. He reveals himself as angry, not a good therapeutic strategy, yet he helps Job listen, perhaps for the first time. He arrives late on the scene, but speaks for six long chapters: in ancient Hebrew culture, Job's silence means he has nothing to say.

Despite Elihu's anger and arrogance, despite his bias against Job, despite his heavy orthodox theology stressing God's transcendence, he moves Job not just toward recovery but toward transformation. Through Elihu, we learn important steps to help improve our communication with people who experience trauma or tragedy. In the same way that Beverly's evaluator helped her listen through the fog of self-preoccupied depression, Elihu's speeches reveal important strengths to help Job—and us—listen.

STRENGTHS: WHAT JOB HEARS

Elihu Addresses Job by Name

> But now, Job, listen to my words (Job 33:1).

Several times throughout his speeches, Elihu addresses Job by name. In the above verse, he does so as part of his legal summons. He concludes that chapter by saying, "Pay heed, Job, and hear me" (33:31). At another point he invites: "Give ear to this, Job" (37:14). Although Elihu shows little interest in Job's emotional suffering but is primarily concerned with legal process,[2] his address to Job by name improves on the speeches of the three friends. They never spoke Job's name. Their simple goal was to goad him to repent. But by addressing Job directly, by name, Elihu pays attention to him as a person. He takes Job and his request for an arbiter seriously.

Elihu Quotes Job's Words

> Indeed, you have stated in my hearing, I heard the words spoken, "I am guiltless, free from transgression; I am innocent, without iniquity. But [God] finds reasons to oppose me, considers me His enemy. He puts my feet in stocks, watches all my ways" (Job 33:8–11).

In an effort to use Job's own words against him, Elihu takes pains to quote what he heard Job say. A silent participant to the previous dialogues, Elihu's quotes of Job are, however, not totally accurate. It is true that Job says, "I am blameless" (9:21) and "Until I die I will maintain my integrity" (27:5). With these statements, however, Job claims not sinless perfection but unjustified suffering:[3] "How many are my iniquities and sins? Advise me of my transgression and sin," Job challenges God in chapter 13.

In the next chapter, on God's distance from people, Elihu opposes Job's words directly. "Surely it is false that God does not listen, that Shaddai does not take note of it. Though you say, 'You do not take note of it,' the case is before Him; so wait for Him" (35:13-14).

Elihu cites Job not only to Job but also to the others. In his first speech defending God's justice (chapter 34), Elihu speaks to the gathered "wise men" at court and, in Job's own words, lays out his complaint. "For Job has said, 'I am right; God has deprived me of justice. I declare the judgment against me false; my arrow-wound is deadly, though I am free from transgression'" (34:5-6). In verse 9, he quotes Job again: "For [Job] says, 'Man gains nothing when he is in God's favor.'"

Even if, by quoting Job, Elihu uses a strategy common to wisdom teachers, it nevertheless helps Job feel Elihu is trying to understand him. Elihu's self-understanding, his impetuousness, and his theology lead him to strongly disagree with Job. Elihu, nevertheless, seems to try to reach out to Job. Even if to refute him, by quoting Job Elihu demonstrates: I hear you. Because he lessens the gap between them, Job continues to listen.

In any disagreement, feeling you are *being heard* reduces tension. After listening to the other person's views, it's important to articulate your friend's position *before* you outline your own. This doesn't mean you agree, of course, just that you understand what the other person is saying. Elihu makes clearer his disagreement with Job.

Elihu Tells Job He Is Wrong

In this you are not [in the legal] right (Job 33:12).

Elihu is adamant: Job errs not only in complaining that God was unjust, but also in his misdirected efforts to summon God into court. "Why do you complain against [God] that He does not reply to any of man's charges" (33:13)? Defending God's distance to the colleagues, Elihu says, "He has no set time for man to appear before God in judgment" (34:23). Note that although Elihu disagrees with Job on almost every score, he does so openly. Contrast him with how the three friends *insinuate* that Job must have sinned to bring his disasters down upon him; that he risks siding with the wicked and must repent. Also note how, in contrast to his friends, Elihu's open disagreement with Job— far more straightforward—promotes healthy communication.

How to disagree while maintaining our relationship at times demands consummate skill. Sometimes we don't say anything to avoid further dissension. Other times, to be true to ourselves, we must express disagreement; we agree to disagree.

Elihu Listens Carefully

If you (Job) can, answer me; argue against me, take your stand (Job 33:5).

In the above challenge, Elihu uses legal terms: "answer," "argue," and "take your stand." Admittedly he wants to rebut Job's complaints. Nevertheless, as arbiter in a legal proceeding, he takes pains to listen to Job to a degree Job's friends fail to do. Because Elihu addresses Job in Job's terms, Job feels better understood. Many comparison passages could be cited. Here is one author's analysis of Elihu's response to Job's legal language:

> Job had challenged God to appear in court, whether as plaintiff or defendant (13:19-22). Elihu takes up that challenge in place of God.
>
> Job had cried, "I will press charges and you refute me" (13:22). Elihu replies, "I am summoning you. You refute me if you can" (33:1, 5).
>
> Job stated that he has prepared his case (13:18). Elihu presumptuously orders Job to "present it before me" (33:5).
>
> Job had established two conditions for a fair trial: no heavy celestial hand and no divine terror to intimidate mortals (13:21). Gratuitously, Elihu advises Job that he need not be overawed by his terror or heavy hand (33:7). After all, he concedes, they are both human.
>
> Job demanded a bill of particulars specifying the charges (13:22). Elihu responds by interpreting Job's case as a plea of total innocence and purity (33:9), and as a charge of oppression and injustice against God (33:10-11).
>
> Job asserted that he is "in the right" (13:18). Elihu condescendingly replies, "I would be delighted to find you in the right" (33:32).[4]

As a beginning pastoral counselor, I learned from the Rev. Jack Hall, one of my supervisors, to stop rephrasing what my client says into my own words. Instead, I needed to learn to use the terms and phrases my client used when describing their distress. Elihu addresses Job's complaints in the legal language Job uses. Again, if we can do that, we reduce conflict by helping the other person feel, *he hears me.*

Elihu Points Job to God

> *Now, then, one cannot see the sun, though it be bright in the heavens, until the wind comes and clears them (of clouds).*

The splendor about God is awesome. Shaddai—we cannot attain to Him;
He is great in power and justice and abundant in righteousness; He does not torment. Therefore men are in awe of Him whom none of the wise can perceive (Job 37:22–24).

In the conclusion to his chapters, Elihu focuses Job's mind on the splendor, majesty, and grandeur of God in creation. He calls God *Shaddai*—"Almighty." "Give ear to this, Job; stop to consider the marvels of God," he says of the clouds and the wind. "Can you soar like Him to Heaven, firm as a mirror of cast metal?" he asks. In the next few verses and throughout the passage above, Elihu attempts to turn Job from his problems by an appeal to God's majesty.

At first such a strategy was counterproductive, as the friends who tried it found. Job was too angry—with God. Job also had no question about God's majesty. The friends missed the point; it was God's ruthless attack on Job through tragedy to which Job objects. Now, however, Job has "vented his spleen," i.e., discharged his hostility, voiced his most negative emotions. He's said everything he can say. More importantly, having also grieved, Job is in a different place. He now can listen.

Elihu attempts one last time to dissuade Job from believing he could force God into court, one last comment to turn Job's heart toward awe of God, whom not even the wise can "see." If he finally accepts Elihu's argument, Elihu believes, Job can be at peace. Even though Job's quest remains unfulfilled, he has done his best; he has done everything he knows, including grieving. He can rest his case. "The case is before Him," Elihu assures Job, "so wait for Him" (35:14). Finally, through Elihu we also find an example of one of the most important ingredients we need for recovery and transformation—offering the sufferer common ground.

OFFERING COMMON GROUND

For God speaks time and again—though man does not perceive it—in a dream
... Then He opens men's understanding, and by disciplining them leaves His signature to turn men away from an action, to suppress pride in man. [God] spares from the Pit... [the person] is reproved by pains on his bed... If [the person] has a representative... to declare the man's uprightness, then [God] has mercy on him and decrees, "Redeem him from descending to the Pit, for I have obtained his ransom" (Job 33:14–24).

In the prevailing view of the friends, Job's suffering results from personal sin. Eliphaz adds in chapter 5, however, that suffering is a form of the Almighty's discipline. Elihu picks up Eliphaz's premature, but somewhat more compassionate, approach. According to Elihu, God uses suffering, along with dreams and an angelic mediator, to repeatedly speak to people. He describes a person suffering from depression and physical illness, and near death. Just then a mediator, perhaps an angel, mercifully intervenes. God declares, "Redeem him from descending to the Pit, for I have obtained his ransom." God accepts the person's suffering as sufficient ransom. After prayer and recovery, the person joins other worshippers: "He enters His presence with shouts of joy" (v. 26). It is then that Elihu, perhaps, springs a trap, for he has the healed person say, "I have sinned; I have perverted what was right; but I was not paid back for it" (v. 27). Elihu's sinner recovers, *then repents*! On the one hand, Job is not required to repent before healing. On the other, Job was to take note and repent after recovery. God may graciously heal first. Elihu's sequence of events, though still objectionable to Job, comes closer to satisfying Job, than that of his friends.

In the end, Elihu still insists Job is in the wrong, but his position on suffering softens. God's discipline of suffering serves as the propitiatory sacrifice ("ransom") for the sufferer. *After* recovery, the sufferer confesses he perverted what was right (pride) yet escaped punishment. God's mercy overrules. Because Job still maintains his innocence, he would still refuse to repent even after recovery, but here is a new way through his dilemma, based on God's mercy. Job would not admit he had perverted the right, not yet at least, but now he can entertain the possibility that, in some way, he might need to repent.

Common Ground, Confrontation, Compassion

Elihu serves an important role in Job's recovery. Despite his faults, he forces Job to listen. It is not unusual for God to use an imperfect human instrument to prepare someone for a later, more direct, confrontation. Ascetic John the Baptist prepares the way for Jesus, eating and drinking, a friend of sinners. A dying Stephen, with Christ-like forgiveness, prepares the way for Saul's dramatic conversion. A court-appointed psychologist served that role for Nicky Cruz, a violent New York gang-leader.

When Nicky appeared before the judge, the arresting officer recalled his two prior appearances. "These kids have killed three officers in the last two years, and we've had almost fifty murders down there since I've been on that beat. The only thing they respond to is force. And I know that if you turn him loose, you're going to have to lock him back up again—only the next time it will probably be for murder," the officer said.[5]

Despite his seeming incorrigibility, the judge gave Nicky one last chance. He assigned him to Dr. John Goodman, the court-appointed psychologist.

After Nicky's initial failed attempt to push the limits with this veteran of the gangs and the Marines, Dr. Goodman "examined" him on a pleasure drive to upstate New York. Instead of returning him to jail, however, Dr. Goodman dropped him back at his housing project, his prerogative. Nicky felt delighted, but Dr. Goodman acted dead sober. He explained that he didn't think jail would do Nicky any good—nothing would.

"Nicky," he said, "I'll give it to you straight. You're doomed. There's no hope for you. And unless you change, you're on a one-way street to jail, the electric chair, and hell."[6]

"Those words kept running through my mind like a stuck record. You're on a one-way street to jail, the electric chair, and hell," Nicky said. "I had never looked at myself before. Not really... But inside I suddenly felt dirty." [7]

Soon after, Nicky attended a David Wilkerson gospel meeting and turned his life over to Christ.

Job stands as a monument not only to recovery from tragedy, but also to transformation.

HOW TO
ASSESS YOUR RECOVERY

1. Review your recovery. Think of your emotional state after your tragedy. What did you have to overcome to get where you are now? Celebrate your accomplishments.

2. How did you survive? What or who helped you? How have you expressed thanks to God and/or other people for their part in helping you survive? What could you do to express your gratitude?

3. How did you accomplish your recovery? What negative emotions did you have to overcome? How similar/different was your recovery from Job's? What lessons from Job were most important for you? How did his experience make a difference for you?

4. What is your greatest need now? What have people said that you've dismissed but now have begun to rethink? How can you thank them for their help?

How to
Help a Friend Recover

You may tire of listening to your loved ones or friends repeat accounts of their losses, but it is critical that you take them seriously. Whether they entertain suicidal thoughts or dismiss their situation as if everything is okay, if someone you love complains unendingly about life and suffering and how unfair it is and why is God doing this to them, address their specific feelings: take them seriously. If necessary, help them get treatment.

A good counselor listens carefully. When the friend or counselor accumulates sufficient evidence, for example at least three similar statements, he or she may, matter-of-factly but gently, confront the client with their own words. "You know I love you, but you've said at least three times...What do you mean? Help me understand." This may help sufferers see the extremes of their emotions and face themselves in a new way.

A caring friend or good counselor may disagree with the sufferer. If so, there must be no hidden agenda, but honest communication. "You haven't heard a word I've said!" the nurse told Beverly. Because that confrontation was honest and healthy, however, it helped her.

Professional counselors listen to what is said, to what is not said, and in what tone of voice. They keep good notes with exact quotations, usually written after the meeting. These are a source of recall to prepare for the next visit. Especially important are the metaphors the sufferer uses to describe their life, loss, conflict, or situation. Do they describe their problems as climbing a mountain, spiritual warfare, or being run over by a truck?

Here are some specific steps:

1. Identify the blunders Elihu makes that you avoided. Which blunders of his did you copy? How could you do better with the next person in tragedy in the future?

2. Practice the counseling techniques of Elihu best suited to increase better communication. Be sure to demonstrate genuine concern for your friend's welfare; don't just use techniques as tricks.

3. Identify what approaches seem to work better than others with your friend. Remember, you may need to take the initiative to reach out. How willing are you to do that?

4. Where have you practiced exploration of common ground in reaching out to someone in tragedy? Are there important messages you need to convey?

5. Encourage those in tragedy by telling them ways you've seen them overcome obstacles in their recovery. One key way to encourage them is to help them reflect on how they've grown in their relationship with God.

CHAPTER 11

GOD'S TRANSFORMING PERSPECTIVE

GETTING TO THIS point in your recovery hasn't been easy. You've waded through a series of negative emotions—depression, for example, anger, and grief. Grieving hasn't been easy, either, but once you've acknowledged the deep sadness, you may have felt the emotional pain begin to lift.

Learning to grieve your tragedies may also have enabled you to listen to others' counsel. Some offered you simple answers to complex problems, but others enabled you to see your loss in a new light. Aware of significant ways you've overcome the worst effects of your tragedy, you may be ready for new perspective.

PLACING PAIN IN PERSPECTIVE

As I lay on the outpatient gurney for a prostate biopsy, I learned how perspective helps us endure pain. Although my memory of the experience has faded, the sharp, stabbing physical pain I felt deep inside my body nearly overwhelmed me. Over and over, despite the verbal and mental preparation to "Get ready," at times I still wanted to cry: six jabs on the left side of my prostate, five on the right. I wasn't counting but when the doctor said, "Only three more…Only two more…Only one more," I couldn't wait for the procedure to end. With each jab I experienced more pain than I ever experienced.

I could have felt angry. I could have quit. I could have run. My urologist standing over my prone body, however, put my pain in perspective: "We want to make sure there's no cancer," he said. He showed me the ultrasound image. He performed that biopsy preliminary to a second procedure that could bring me permanent relief, but cancer would have ruled that procedure out. Several days later, his office called with the pathology results—negative. Good news!

Thankfully, at eleven jabs, my biopsy ended. I suffered, but the context was my greater good: Did I have a malignancy? My pain felt excruciating, but at least it had meaning. That was Job's big complaint at the start—he saw no meaning to his tragedy. The way he put it in chapter 3, God has "hedged me in."

Although we know the meaning of Job's suffering, like him, many times we don't know the meaning of our own. After working through our grief, indeed as part of it, finding meaning, purpose, and perspective for our suffering presents our greatest single challenge. Without it, we rage against our impersonal but unjust fate or our personal but angry God. With perspective we can recover.

Job speaks for us all in tragedy. His questions are just as timely, just as relevant, and just as compelling as our own: they *are* our own. We can't wait to hear God's response to Job's innocent suffering. We anticipate some explanation, but when we hear what God says, we feel baffled at how neatly he seems to sidestep Job's question and ours: "Why?"

Breaking His Silence

Throughout the dialogues between Job and his friends, God remains silent. Instead of rushing in to correct Job in the midst of his depression, where Job reinterprets statements of his friends negatively, or in his terrifying paranoia, where His approach would only intensify Job's fear, God waits. He also waits until Job has time to mourn his losses. Finally, God waits until Job shows an ability to listen.

Job wants God to inform him of his sin, or to allow him to submit his complaint of injustice. But when God does speak, His response based in reality represents strong medicine. With some justification, people have criticized God's speeches as *too* strong, as bullying, or as telling Job to "Shut up!" (See 38:4–5, 21) In fact, in these chapters, God answers fifteen specific charges Job levels.[1] Confronting Job earlier with reality as God sees it could have pushed him deeper into despair.

We can understand God's speeches also in the context of counseling. In the first several sessions, a counselor listens carefully, gathers information, and shows feeling for the client. As counseling progresses, the counselor becomes less a passive listener, and more an active co-strategist. In the struggle to help the client grapple with tragedy, sooner or later the counselor needs to help the counselee face the reality of changed circumstances. Empathetic listening, while vital at the beginning, is not adequate to help the client deal effectively with tragedy.

In a climate of trust the client needs to face reality: my child is dead, my marriage is over, my illness likely will take my life, or I will have to live with my mental disability the rest of my life. Such a message is never easy to hear, but as the reality slowly dawns, a counselee may show readiness to deal with such news realistically. After grieving the loss, planning for a changed life and anticipating the future come into focus. The counselor may now offer to help explore the reality of the changed situation, with strategies for coping. Coming to terms with reality transforms us.

When God graciously offers him an audience in a tornado, Job feels awed by God's presence. Moreover, he feels overwhelmed with what God says about reality as He frames Job's suffering within His perspective as Creator. God's response to our questions through Job also provides us transformative perspective. Answers to such important questions as: *Who is God? Does He speak? If so, when?* and *What does He say?* all play a vital role in Job's transformation. Those answers play an equally important role in ours.

PERSPECTIVE: WHO IS GOD?

Then the Lord replied to Job out of the tempest (Job 38:1).

Nowhere must we define our terms more carefully than with God's name. Throughout the speeches with his friends, they and Job refer to God as the Almighty, God the Creator: *El, Eloah,* and *Shaddai.* Those generic terms for God refer to His creative power and transcendent majesty.

But recall the narrator's description of the heavenly courtroom, where "the Lord" reigns. And in his initial response to his losses Job praises "the Lord." That name is reserved for the personal God of Abraham, Isaac, and Jacob, the deity worshipped in Israel. As the Lord in a volcanic eruption reveals Himself to His people with Moses in Israel's earlier theophany (manifesting of a deity; Exodus 19:18), He now reveals Himself in person to Job. By responding to his request at long last, the Lord graciously honors Job. In chapter 38, therefore, with a surprise of His sovereign grace, the Lord, the personal God of Israel, breaks through to speak to lowly Job.[2]

In tragedy, especially in depression, as with Job, we may lose our sense of God's presence so that *we feel* God as distant, silent, and absent. For some God ceases to exist. Anthony Flew, world-famous British philosopher, recently turned from agnosticism (not knowing whether God exists) toward theism, a belief in a divine being. Because of the presence of evil, however, he says he can't believe in a personal deity.[3]

Because of evil we may also find belief in the personal God of Job difficult to accept. Life can seem like a relentless cycle of impersonal events: life and death, sickness and health, tragedy and survival. Where do we see God intervene? Even more difficult is the presence of evil, but the Lord's response to Job also helps to answer Flew's objection: God's creation at present includes evil. As He does for Job, the Lord may also be gracious to you to reveal who He is.

PERSPECTIVE: DOES GOD SPEAK?

Then the Lord replied to Job out of the tempest. Job 38:1

God's sudden appearance out of a tornado surprises us. After Job exhausts all his arguments, when his "case" seems hopeless, and after he gives up, God speaks. Have you tried to summon God? Have you prayed and prayed for God to intervene, only to be forced to yield to His silence? Have you exhausted every avenue of redress, only to relinquish hope of healing? That has also been my temptation with our daughter-in-law Juli's chronic illnesses. Periodically, nevertheless, the Lord reminds me to pray for her freedom from pain, or for grace for her to sustain her in her pain—for today.

I can't predict when or how God will speak to you—or if He will. I only know that when Job least expected it, God graciously spoke to him out of a storm. I do know God spoke through the Hebrew prophets. I do know He speaks today through Jesus Christ and the Holy Spirit. At times He speaks through a miraculous healing; at other times He speaks to us through caring people who share their concern; at still other times He speaks through a passage of Scripture. Sometimes He speaks with a gentle nudge of insight; at other times, as He did with Job, He overwhelms us with His power. Because He is sovereign, we never know when or whether He will intervene. But we can anticipate, pray, and remain open.

P<small>ERSPECTIVE</small>: W<small>HEN</small> D<small>OES THE</small> L<small>ORD</small> S<small>PEAK</small>?

In chapter after chapter Job pleads, complains, cajoles, and even sues God to force Him to respond. That effort seems hopeless: God refuses. "The words of Job are ended," says the narrator at the end of Job's last-ditch effort at a response, his *affidavit* in chapter 31. By this time, Job has given up. There is nothing more to say. In the chapters immediately before the Lord's speech, Elihu makes plain that Job has no right to expect God to respond: "He has no set time for man to appear before God in judgment" (34:23). In addition, the last words of Elihu in chapter 37 also stress the futility of Job's petition. "Shaddai—we cannot attain to Him; He is great in power and justice and abundant in righteousness; He does not pervert [i.e., justice]."⁴ God's majesty, creative marvels, and transcendence (chapter 35), make meaningless Job's hope for a meeting. Beyond the ability of mortals to speak with Him in person, God transcends human categories, including a courtroom.

When we look at ourselves, we see that our circumstances haven't changed, our prayers have gone unanswered, and our questions remain. Like Job we may have given up. We've given up pressuring God to respond to our need. When we've done all the praying we can, when we've said everything worth saying, when others have exhausted all the comfort, consolation, and confronting they can think of, God remains silent. We long for Him to speak, but will He?

When God responds, He does so out of grace. When He does respond He does so in His time, in His way, and for His glory. Of course, the Lord is under no obligation to respond to our needs, prayers, or petitions. Job needs to learn that lesson of ceding control. Immediately after his tragedies, Job said the right words: "The Lord gives and the Lord takes away."

For so many reasons, the Lord chose to wait Job out until he is ready. That may well be one reason He hasn't answered *our* petitions.

PERSPECTIVE: WHAT DOES THE LORD SAY?

When the Lord finally responds to Job, He counters with challenges—challenges strong enough to overwhelm Job. The Lord challenges Job's ignorance, understanding of the natural world, understanding of the animal world, and Job's ability to contain chaos. In the process, the Lord addresses his resentment over unjust suffering.

Challenges Job's Ignorance: Who Are You?

> *Who is this who darkens counsel [literally "design"], speaking without knowledge? (Job 38:2).*

On the basis of his ignorance of the Lord's design, the Lord challenges Job's standing. Job's bitter complaints, though not sin as his friends believed, reveal ignorance of the Lord's plan of creation. Along with his friends, Job assumes a correlation between a righteous life and material blessing. That assumption, the basis of his many complaints about how the Lord runs the world, obscures the Lord's design. The specifics of that plan the Lord soon explains. In the meantime, our world, our life, rules for reward, owe us nothing. When I expect God to reward my righteousness and punish evildoers, my suffering is as likely to cloud the Lord's plan as Job's. My ignorance shows.

In the process of honoring Job, and us, with His presence and revelation, the Lord also challenges—hard. "Gird up your loins like a man," He tells Job in v. 3. "I will ask and you will inform Me." Job must now grow up, act like a true warrior, admit his ignorance of the Lord's design, and prepare to do verbal battle.[5]

Challenges Job's Understanding: The Natural World

> *Where were you when I laid the earth's foundations? Do you know who fixed its dimensions? (Job 38:4–5).*

In his cross-examination of the plaintiff, the Lord reveals Himself as the Sovereign, All-powerful Creator. Question after question cascades over Job, each one as unanswerable as the one before. Where were you? Do you know? Who set (the world's) cornerstone? Who closed the sea? Have you ever commanded the dawn to break? Have you penetrated to the recesses of the (ocean) deep? Have you surveyed the expanses of the earth? With sarcasm, the Lord pauses long enough to ask, "If you know of these—tell Me." That design of creation balances control with freedom. On the one hand, the Lord controls by ordering the heavenly constellations according to natural laws (38:31–33). On the other, the Lord freely intervenes by special ordering daybreak (38:12), sending hail (38:22–23), pouring rain, and dispatching lightning (38:34–35).

The Lord now draws closer to Job's challenge of injustice. He explains His design with regard to wicked and evil people. As a farmer shakes out chaff from his lap, when the Lord's dawn breaks, He seizes the earth by its corners, and shakes out the wicked (38:12–13). As a result of the new day's light, "the upright arm is broken"(38:15). Although the wicked rule under cover of darkness, the Lord's dawn exposes, limits, and prevents further violence. In comparison, how adept is Job to control the wicked?

Like an infant who rages when she realizes the world does not revolve around her, so Job, even with his righteous behavior, rages to learn he is not immune to disaster. The Lord reminds Job that

He, the Lord, created the earth, controls the sea, breaks the dawn, guards the gates of death, manages the weather, binds the constellations, and discharges the lightning. They operate according to His plan, within limits He sets, according to times He controls, and obey laws He institutes. The Lord also reminds Job that order limits chaos. "You may come so far and no farther; here your surging waves will stop" (38:11), the Lord says of the ocean. Although limited, the Lord's design, then, includes both order *and* chaos.[6]

At times we may feel omnipotent. We are innocent; others are guilty. We are right; others wrong. We are just; others are evildoers. When we've experienced tragedy, we're so overwhelmed with our suffering that we can even accuse God. When we do, we lose perspective. The Lord's response to Job helps us balance the good with evil.

Challenges Job's Understanding: The Animals

Do you know the season when the mountain goats give birth?
Can you mark the time when the hinds calve? (Job 29:1).

The Lord then follows those impossible questions about physical nature with questions about animal creation to which Job must again answer, "No, I don't know." "Do you know when mountain goats birth their young?" the Lord asks. "Can you hunt prey for the lion? Who sets the wild ass free? Do you give the horse his strength? Does the eagle soar at your command?" The Lord reminds Job that in His design the animals function through balance. Some animals such as lions and ravens prey on other animals for food. In fact, hungry ravens "cry out to God." For lions and ravens to live, other creatures die. God provides their food. Compare that with the next illustration: "Do you know the season when the mountain goats give birth?" Life among the animals goes on, just as death, without Job. Without Job's help or ability to control, new life balances death.

I recently attended a family wedding, with all the joy, celebration, and hope such events bring. I thought of how often a family funeral also draws families together. Balancing our funerals and memorial services, then, weddings, births, promotions, graduations, and achievements provide needed balance to offset our times of sadness.

Another lesson Job should draw from the animals: their freedom, both from human control, and in their own right. They give birth and die in their own world. The hind grows up in the open, and then leaves the doe to return no more (39:1-4). "Who sets the wild ass free?" the Lord also wants to know. "Who loosens the bonds of the onager" (39:5)? Because of temperament, people find the onager, a wild ass, impossible to domesticate.[7] Not only does the hawk not fly by Job's wisdom (39:26), the eagle (probably vulture, since its young gulps blood 39:30) does not soar "at your command."

The basis of Job's protest, and also his friends' beliefs, focused on their rigid application of a doctrine of retribution: God always rewards the righteous and always punishes the unrighteous. Throughout these passages, the Lord makes plain that such a belief makes Him subject to arbitrary, man-made, control. Instead, the Lord of Creation imbued His handiwork with incredible freedom. Nowhere in creation does such a doctrine of retribution apply. When we protest the Lord's treatment of our lives, we easily lose sight of this principle of freedom. The universe does not revolve around human beings, or around our needs. The complex nature of the Lord creates a complex life, full of ways to harness nature, and ways nature eludes our control.

Surprisingly, the Lord's design for the world includes not only peace, but also war. In contrast to the tranquil mountain goats and deer, the horse, oblivious to the danger of arrows, sword, or javelin, charges into battle. Drawn by the scent of warfare, he relishes the trumpet, and snorts, "Aha!" (39:19-25). Like the horse, some human warriors relish combat. Despite tragic death of our children and parents in warfare, life goes on.

The hawk and vulture demonstrate not only freedom, but also "wisdom" in their ability to soar. Though not because of Job's wisdom, the hawk, for example, grows long wings. "Does the eagle soar at your command?" the Lord also asks Job (39:27). Does Job command it to build his nest high, spy his food, and feed his young on the slain (39:26-30)? The folly-ridden ostrich, by contrast, leaves her eggs in danger on the ground, and cruelly abandons her young. All her labor goes for nothing because "God deprived her of wisdom" (39:13-18).

The Lord's plan for creation balances death with life, chaos with order, control with freedom, evil with good, war with peace, and folly with wisdom. That balance creates mystery, paradox, conflicting interests, needs, and struggle. The Lord pursues His purposes within that design of His creation. With Job, the Lord challenges us to adopt a new perspective on evil in the light of the paradoxes of His creation. [8]

Challenges Job's Control: The Reality of Chaos

> *Take now Behemoth, whom I made as I did you (Job 40:15).*
> *Can you draw out Leviathan by a fishhook? (Job 40:25).*

Our understanding of what is just, right, or fair does not bind the Lord. To demonstrate further that His world contains elements humans cannot control, the Lord presents Job, and us, with Behemoth and Leviathan. We feel shocked that the Lord created Behemoth as He did Job! In fact, he is the "first of God's works" (literally "ways" v. 19a). His strength and prowess are so intimidating, "only his Maker can draw the sword against him" (v. 19b). Behemoth does as he pleases: lounges in the lotus, restrains the river, and, should he move, creates a gushing stream. The Lord asks Job to look at Behemoth, observe, and learn.

The Lord then continues Job's grinding cross-examination. Can that beast Leviathan be "taken by the eyes, or his nose pierced by hooks" (v. 24)? The answer again is, "No, of course not." The Lord confronts Job with, for humans, raw, uncontrollable power. Yet that power is the Lord's creation, built into earliest reality that only his Creator can control. There are some situations over which you and I have control, but many others over which we have no control. Learning to live within our limits tests our character. We hate to admit that an accident, tornado, hurricane, drought, or violence can snatch a beloved's life—or our own.

At even greater length, with more detail, and with more unanswerable questions, the Lord further barrages Job about Leviathan (40:25–41:26). In chapter 3 Job wants others to rouse Leviathan, the fearful chaos monster of the deep, to cast a death spell on the day of his birth. Big mistake! No one is fierce enough to rouse him (41:10). This monstrous sea-dragon, as with the hippopotamus-like Behemoth, you can't capture, i.e., control. That's the message of the Lord's unanswerable questions in verses 41:1-11. In fact, touch him "and you will never think of battle again" (v. 8). Just the sight of him induces prostration (v. 9).

Here the Lord turns the attention to Himself. If you can't capture/control Leviathan, "Who, then can stand up to Me? Whoever confronts Me, I will requite, for everything under the heavens is Mine" (41:2-3). Even Leviathan is the Lord's?

Job miscalculates the nature of reality; he also misjudges the Almighty Lord. Just as Job said he would not be silent or restrained in his complaint in chapter 7, the Lord now says He will not be silent about Leviathan.[9] With continued withering cross-examination, the Lord presses His counter-case against Job. Question after question about Leviathan confront Job with the impossibility of Job's control.

Leviathan's defensive armament makes him invulnerable (41:13-17). His fire-breathing aggression makes him dangerous (vv. 18-21). His strength, power, and toughness show in his neck and flesh (vv. 22-23). His heart is as hard as stone and just as cold (v. 24). Even divine beings stand in dread of him (v. 25). Launch an arsenal of weapons against him: sword, spear, missile, lance, iron, bronze, arrow, sling stone, club, and javelin and you find them useless (vv. 26-29). He has no soft underbelly to attack (v. 30). Like the prow of an ocean liner at night, the sea seethes in his motion to create a wake of luminosity (vv. 31-32).

Therefore, "no one on land can dominate him made as he is without fear" (v. 33). That means Job. That means you and me. Therefore, also, we are humbled before him, this uncontrollable beast of chaos, evil, destruction, and death. "He sees all that is haughty (Job? Me?); he is king over all proud beasts" (v. 34). If Leviathan reigns over all proud beasts, where does that leave us humans?

After reading this passage, I feel overwhelmed. Once again, the book conveys an experience of the Lord. Reading this description confronts us with destructive, terrifying, uncontrollable chaos. I must not think I am up to taming the beast. I stand helpless, humbled, and laughed at—humiliated. We all do.

We can rail against the Lord for His injustice, but that's the world He made, full of joy, power, and freedom, but also full of uncontrollable evil, destruction, and death. The Lord is just, but He's given us a complex world, with contradictions, paradoxes, and dangers. We do our best against forces arrayed against us, but ultimately entrust our lives to Him. Only the Lord's overwhelming power controls our chaos.

"NOT THE ANSWER I EXPECTED"

The Lord's series of speeches confounds our expectations, as it did Job's. We expect understanding, sympathy, and warmth from the Lord over our tragic losses. Instead, the Lord blasts us with unanswerable questions, exposes our ignorance, and confronts us with images of overwhelming power. The message: It's time you face a world that produces disaster as well as blessing. At one of my presentations of this passage to members of his congregation, my pastor friend rose to express his frustration. "That wasn't the answer I expected," he said. We expect the Lord to show us more understanding; instead He reveals the raw truth about life. Another pastor wrote of the response of his congregation to this passage. "(God's response)...made some uncomfortable, but it is reality. God's ways are not our own." God's ways are different. If it were up to us, we'd live like the main character in the movie *Bruce Almighty*, with everything going our way all the time. But even with omnipotence, Bruce ran into complications.

Isn't it time for you to face what you've experienced: the trauma, the tragedy, the disaster, and the forces beyond your control? The cost of continued denial is exorbitant in lost ability to function, in poorer relationships, and in lowered self-esteem. If you have difficulty turning away from your tragedy, you may have more grief or trauma to work through. The ability to sort out what you can control (ourselves, our responses) from what you can't (events, other people) takes wisdom.

Facing reality is difficult, but it brings rewards. It enables us to move beyond our loss to rebuild new lives. Having loved, lost, and reconciled with our suffering, we can become emotionally stronger. We can better understand, sympathize with, and help others in similar circumstances. We empathize with the suffering of innocent people around the world: Cambodians, Rwandans, Jewish victims of the Holocaust, and persecuted Christians. Facing reality transforms us into more complete individuals, at peace with a world in conflict.

How to
Face Reality

1. Admit the difficulty of this step. If you're still in denial, confront it; admit your true emotions to yourself, to a trusted friend or counselor, and to God. Ask God for strength to grasp the reality you face and to help you resolve your loss.

2. Identify your denial. Denial says, "I don't see it, I don't want to see it, and I don't want you to tell me about it." What is it that you have the hardest time facing? How have you shut out friends and loved ones? What would it take for you to reverse course and welcome their perspective? How would you signal your openness?

3. Suffering drove Job away from a feeling of close fellowship with the Lord. Identify ways your suffering has affected your relationship with Him.

4. List some ways you can love and serve the Lord in the face of, despite, and/or in the midst of your tragedy.

5. Given the kind of world we inhabit (with tragedy as well as blessing), practice worshipping God "for nothing" (without expectation of reward), because of Who He is: Worthy. That was Satan's challenge to the Lord about Job (1:9; 2:3), that he worshipped the Lord only because of the blessings he received. With Job, prove Satan wrong—again.

CHAPTER 12

TRANSFORMING YOUR TRAGEDY

As a result of your willingness to undertake this journey, I hope you've taken at least one major step forward in your recovery. Although you may have a distance to go, looking back on where you started can help you appreciate how far you've come. It can provide the courage necessary to overcome the lingering denial we feel when events force us to confront our loss. It also can encourage continued openness to what God offers in our new reality.

How Far Have I Come?

As you recall your recovery from tragedy, what do you see? Do you remember those times of despair over the meaning of your life? Where is that despair now? Do you find that such times gradually lessened in frequency? Yes, you have them, but perhaps there is now a lot more time in between. Instead of a blue period every day, you may now go weeks without one. What about their intensity? Do you find that instead of hitting 8 or

9 on a scale of 1 to10, you now reach only 4 or 5? That's a lot of progress to celebrate.

In the same way, how do you gauge your other depressing thoughts, sleepless nights, or downcast mood? Can you point to a lessening of them as well? And your angry thoughts—do you find those have lessened? Do you find you're spending less time blaming God or attributing events to His hostile intervention? Have your spells of grief given way to new activities, relationships, and calmer thoughts? Your recovery may be in full swing. If so, congratulate yourself.

At the same time, you may be ready to reflect more on what you need now. Let me suggest some important matters to consider.

Come to Terms With Reality

Your next order of business may be to face the things about your tragedy that you've denied or avoided. Perhaps you've kept busy to distract yourself from your inner pain, and you still protect a reservoir of hurt. You won't talk about it or let your closest friend bring it up without changing the subject. God confronted Job's sense of injustice with the reality that nowhere in life does righteousness promise to produce material prosperity. Life is indifferent to our particular need for redress of grievances. That was a hard lesson for Job to learn, and you may need to learn similar challenging lessons from your tragedy.

Another common problem is an unrealistic need for closure. Not only have you found no quick fix, you may have discovered no fix at all. Instead you've found it necessary to grieve, grieve, and grieve some more. But after each period of grief, you've experienced periods of relief, which have lengthened and enabled you to cope better. This is normal—painful, but normal.

Perhaps you've reproached yourself for not "getting over it" sooner. I encourage you to treat yourself kindly, to take as long as you need to work through your turmoil, to feel no pressure to be in better emotional shape than you are. Disregard others' expectations; give yourself permission to heal at your own pace. Hank (chapter 9) knew he was on track of his descent into grief and ascent into recovery. The process of overcoming strong negative emotions such as we observed in Job takes time to accomplish. The narrator tells Job's story without any time references. We have no idea how long Job's recovery took, but we can be sure it took longer than the time it takes to read the book. Because even so-called normal grief can create great emotional pain, give yourself time to heal.

Mary retells her tragedy through tears: "When John and I kissed good-bye that morning, I had no idea it would be our last. After John left to take the bus to work, his heart attack came on so suddenly and so severely, that he made no attempt to break his fall. Losing my husband of twenty-years was like having one-half of my personality ripped off—radical amputation."

But that wasn't Mary's only loss. Her second husband, Robert, a PhD in physics worked where he was exposed to asbestos. "Thirteen years after we married, X-ray check-ups for fluid on his lung every three months continued negative, but a follow-up biopsy confirmed cancer." Eight weeks later Robert died.

Mary recalls good years with her husbands, and the joy of raising children. She said those memories release her "from any why questions and from any anger. I never got mad at God when I had two perfect children. I didn't ask Him, 'Why are my kids perfect and other kids have mental health issues or are deformed?' I didn't ask Him why then, so why should I ask Him why now?"

Mary's intense emotional response to her losses did not lead to bitterness or to the need for outside assistance. Despite her grief, crying throughout our conversation, her strong faith and good memories gave her perspective to carry her through dark times.

Consider Professional Help

Some, however may not have the same resources, and may question whether what they experience is unusual or abnormal.

Do you need professional help? How do you determine that? As a rule of thumb, if you have symptoms you can't control, or if disturbing symptoms persist or even increase, that may be your tip-off.

To help assess whether you need a professional's assistance, you may need to distinguish between normal and pathological grief, between trauma in the past and continued re-experiencing in the present, between depression symptoms that you can control and those you can't. Guilt feelings can complicate normal grief. If guilty feelings don't dissipate, you probably need a professional to help you sort them out. If you continue to re-experience a traumatic event or events in the past, you also may need a professional to assist you. Finally, if your depressed and/or suicidal thoughts fail to lessen, or if they intensify, you should seek professional help.

A *professional counselor* specializes in helping people overcome difficulties. Through careful investigation of the origins and symptoms of what you experience, counselors work with you to draw up a plan to address the most distressing symptoms. Just the experience of speaking with a trusted and confidential advisor can relieve your anxiety to a great extent. Through patient listening, counselors can help you develop strategies to reduce your most difficult symptoms. They will work toward enabling you to solve your own conflicts, make your own decisions, and generally empower you to take better control of your life. Several types of counselors are available today. Each subscribes to a specific set of ethical guidelines that are available to read on their web sites.

A *licensed professional counselor* (LPC) has been trained and licensed in your state to provide counseling services. Usually holding a Master's degree in counseling, the LPC can work with you on emotional and mental issues but must refer you to a psychiatrist or psychiatric nurse practitioner for an evaluation for medication.

Similarly, *a licensed clinical social worker* (LCSW) can provide skilled counseling help, and *a licensed marriage and family therapist* (LMFT) specializes in marriage and family issues. They also will refer you to a psychiatrist or psychiatric nurse practitioner for medication.

A *psychologist* has an advanced degree in the field (PhD or PsyD) and is licensed after examination by the state's licensing board. Some psychologists have been granted authority to prescribe medication, but most must refer.

A *psychiatrist* is a medical doctor (MD) with a specialty in mental disorders. As doctors, they routinely prescribe medication. In fact, many psychiatrists today see patients only for medication; psychologists and other counselors handle the counseling responsibilities.

With both theological and behavioral science training, a *pastoral counselor* usually has served a church or continues to do so. Although any of the other counselors may integrate counseling within a Christian framework, pastoral counselors bring special sensitivity, training, and skills in spiritual as well as psychological issues.

The best way to find a counselor is to ask friends to recommend someone who has helped them. Your pastor, spiritual advisor, or primary care physician also can refer you.

Medication

When you cannot control your symptoms by yourself through strategies that previously worked, you may need medication. Your course of medication may be temporary until your counseling experience enables you to weather your crisis and build strategies to face your life without it. Or you may require medication for an extended period. Different medications prescribed by a psychiatrist or primary care physician can lower your anxiety, reduce suicidal thoughts and depressed feelings, lessen your manic highs, or stop uncontrollable irrational thoughts that intrude and that you cannot stop.

Your counselor may recommend you for an evaluation for medication. This is a routine part of the initial conversation. You may not need medication, but it's best to make that decision in consultation with a medical professional.

Renew Your Relationship With God (42:1-6)

Another helpful strategy to strengthen your recovery is to renew your relationship with God. After his audience with the Lord, Job presents us with several ways to respond to God.

Acknowledge that God Is in Control

> Job said in reply to the Lord:
> I know that You can do everything, that no plan is impossible for You (Job 42:1–2).

In Job's story, God shows His sovereign control from beginning to end: In chapters 1 and 2 He twice limits Satan's ability to harm Job, remains silent in face of Job's most intense provocations, speaks when least expected, addresses Job personally, and says what Job least wants to hear. Perhaps to reflect his suspicion of the Lord's deliberate assault, Job here uses a word for plan ("scheme") with a potentially more insidious meaning than the word used more commonly ("design") in other places in the book.[1] He nevertheless repeats his acknowledgement of the Lord's sovereign control. Whether we see our afflictions as natural consequences or as the result of some hostile intent, we cannot control life. When the Lord does speak, He says what most helps Job find a transforming perspective. "That was my problem," Andrea said (chapter 3). "I was trying to do it all on my own. I wasn't trusting God."

When life becomes chaotic, we question where God is. Only after later reflection do we have to acknowledge how God worked in the most upsetting circumstances. Is that also hard for you to perceive? Are you still struggling in a chaotic period with an uncertain outcome?

Learning what we can control and what we can't can help reduce worry. Giving God those aspects of our lives we can't control can help us live with greater confidence as we do those things for which we have responsibility. That includes our grief, our helplessness, and our other painful emotions. Acknowledging God's sovereign control over all of our life can help us develop a renewed relationship with Him.

When God Speaks, Show You Hear Him

> *[You asked] Who is this who obscures design without knowledge? (Job 42:3).*

Here Job uses the word more commonly used for God's "design" for the universe. Job had pursued justice, but the Lord said that Job was ignorant of the Lord's plan, of pain with blessing. Although this wasn't Job's priority, by quoting the Lord, he shows he "hears" the Lord.

To restate others' view shows we've heard them. Our ability to restate our opponents' views enables us to begin to resolve conflict. "Here is what I hear you saying...Is this correct?" That shows an opponent we understand their position. In conflict, we invest great effort to make sure others understand us. Although we still disagree, when we both show we understand each other's position, the discussion can move more easily to find common ground and resolve the conflict. Until mutual understanding occurs, however, conflict can escalate. Job shows he's heard the Lord's counter-challenge.

Is God speaking to you? Has He spoken to you through the stories I've shared? Through Job's story? If not in a direct, audible way, have you found points of contact with your own story? And what about God using others to speak to you? What are your friends saying? Your family? Your church group members? How does reading the Scriptures each day inform your understanding? What was God's message to His people? How does that apply to you now? Do you pray? When you wait on God, how does He respond? God has many ways to speak to us. We need to show Him that we've heard.

Admit Ignorance

> *Indeed I spoke without understanding of things beyond me, which I did not know (Job 42:3).*

Job's complaints throughout his recovery show how much he "knows:" his innocence, God's injustice, the suffering of the innocent, the prosperity of the wicked, the errors of his colleagues. The Lord never accuses Job of sin but, through his long descriptions of physical nature, animals, and chaos, he does accuse Job of ignorance. Job had sought an audience with God to prove his innocence, but Job's efforts at self-justification, his rhetoric of innocence, and his skewering of God for injustice all went for naught.

Several years ago Juli learned of the plight of a man with increasing disabilities. In response, she wrote him an extended letter that she shared with her family, in which she described her similar experiences, shared her empathy with him, and explained how her illness drew her closer to Jesus. "Since my illness prohibits me from participating in everyday activities like raising children, work, and church life," she wrote, "I'm often haunted with thoughts of 'Why am I here on earth?' and 'What does God want from me anyway?' It's easy to be spiritually hindered by a sense of purposelessness."

Juli wrote of finding her answer in the Apostle Paul, who says, "Offer your bodies as living sacrifices, holy and pleasing to God—*this is your spiritual act of worship*" (Romans 12:1 NIV; emphasis hers). "This is how we fulfill our purpose in life: 'do not conform to this world, but be transformed by the renewing of your mind' (Romans 12:2). The only 'thing that renews my mind about this awful suffering is to refuse to see it as the world sees it but rather to see God's purpose in it. For believers, the sovereign hand of God, to test our faith, orchestrates trials." Her thoughts here closely approximate the author of the Book of Job, where God allows Satan to test Job. In closing, Juli penned a practical perspective for the sufferer to pray:

> Heavenly Father, I have more pain that I know what to do with. I don't understand Your purpose in allowing this kind of suffering in my life. But Your ways are higher than my ways and Your thoughts higher than my thoughts. I will, therefore, do my best within my limits to offer all my time, energy, and will to serve You.

Juli's prayer also may serve as a model for you. To face her suffering squarely, admit her limitations, and seek to serve God within those limitations, Juli's grasp of Scripture transformed her perspective on suffering. While no one would wish such suffering on another, we can admire the quality of her relationship with God that resulted. Difficult as it is, to learn to serve God within the limits He has set for us helps our sense of communion with Him.

What situation do you live with that seems to have no answer? Do you also need to admit your helplessness, ignorance, and inability to control something that has affected your life negatively: a chronic medical condition, a child with a disability, or a spouse with dementia? When we acknowledge God's design with all its ambiguities, disappointments, and setbacks, we gain a better grasp on reality. The sovereignty of God transforms our life from that of a passive victim to that of an active servant. Our relationship with God grows into a deeper, more dependent, and more humble bond.

What You Can Say

[You said] Hear now, and I will speak; I will ask, and you will inform me. I had heard You with my ears, but now I see You with my eyes (Job 42:4-5).

After Job ignores the Lord's double challenge to verbal battle ("Gird up your loins like a man" 38:3; 40:7), he again directly quotes the Lord's words (cf. v. 3 above). Job then says that he has heard the Lord speaking to him.

For Job to "see" God represents Job's highest hope fulfilled. Given his sense of injustice, Job had longed to confront God "face to face." Time and again, however, his longing remains unfulfilled. "But if I go East—He is not there; West—I still do not perceive him; North—since he is concealed, I do not behold him; South—he is hidden, and I cannot see him" (23:8-9; also 19:25-27). As the Lord revealed Himself to Abraham and to Moses, He now grants Job his wish, vindicating him as the hero whose complaints must be addressed.[2] The Lord answers Job's complaints of injustice directly by appeal to the laws of nature rather than those of man-made retribution, not what Job had hoped for. Job's Oath of Integrity in chapter 31, however, also remains intact; Job is innocent. Job acknowledges his direct experience of the Lord, expressed as hearing and seeing Him. Such expressions of communion show a transformed relationship with God: close, personal, and affirming.

WHAT YOU CAN DO

Therefore, I recant and relent, being but dust and ashes (Job 42:6).

Along with Job, we can withdraw our complaint, complete our mourning, and accept consolation from the Lord and from our family and friends.

Now that Job has conceded his ignorance of things too wonderful (too miraculous) for him to understand, and because the Lord appears to him face-to-face, Job relinquishes his protest, including his lawsuit. He once thought he had an "open and shut" case against the Lord for injustice. Now, on the basis of the Lord's word to him, he relinquishes his complaint. What is, is. There is no redress for his—or our—misfortune, nor is there any claim he or we can make on the Lord for our tragedies. I experienced a similar struggle with the injustice of Paul and Juli's illnesses. I recorded my thoughts:

> Today in prayer, the Lord touched me. As I reflected on Job's cry of complaint against God's injustice, I also thought of how he was forced at the end of the book to retract his complaint. I realized that I also had to retract my complaint against God's injustice for Paul and Juli's illness, my resentment, and anger with God. I had to be content with knowing and loving Him better. Tears flooded my eyes. It's hard for me to give up my sense of rightness, my wanting to be right (and God wrong), but there is freedom in letting Him be God and reaching out to Him in love and adoration despite the pain.

Giving up my sense of injustice created in me a cry of mourning. Is that a step you also need to take? Or are you continuing to hold on to the unfairness of it all, to God's (or Life's) injustice to you or to someone you love? Your frustration (anger, rage) changes nothing. It may, in fact, hold you back from learning important lessons from your tragedy. Is it not time for you also to give up your hold on being "right" about God's injustice—and let God be God?

Without guilt for sin from which he needs to repent, Job completes his task of mourning. Only after he fully grieves can he turn away to accept consolation from his colleagues and from the Lord. In response to Job's challenge, the Lord consoles Job through His presence. By relenting Job now signals his willingness to end his mourning.

Have you found consolation? Do you have more grief to express before you can turn away? Are you, perhaps, ready to do so now? Grief itself can transform, as can turning away from mourning our losses. Loss forces change on us. Although such change is painful, we must adjust to the new situation, shoulder the load once shared with a loved one, and make the best of our future. Are you also ready now to turn from your grieving to accept the consolation others, including God, offer?

Finally, like Job, we are "but dust and ashes." We may see ourselves as a hero battling the gates of heaven to seek redress of our grievances, but in reality, we are dust and ashes. Job also accepts consolation for his humbled state of humanness, weakness, and vulnerability to death. He's been seated among dust and ashes since the beginning of his conversations (2:8, 12). Now that he's done everything he can, he yields to his mortality.

Do you need a renewed personal relationship with God? Job's Lord also seeks a personal relationship with you. Your suffering from tragedy, as with Job, can turn God into your enemy and also separate you from Him. But, like Job, as you begin to see your suffering in a more realistic light, you may become more receptive to Him.

Serve Others

Serve others who identify with your story. One woman on my street attends a monthly support group of parents who have lost a child through suicide. She understands their anguish; she knows their grief because she lost her daughter that way. Through her loss, she now helps others; out of her anguish, she can genuinely hear the broken hearts of other parents.

Your tragedy may have prepared you to serve others in similar anguish. What holds you back from finding a place to offer your service to people who've suffered a tragedy similar to yours?

THE PATIENCE OF JOB

People today commonly use the expression, "He has the patience of Job." This phrase comes from the New Testament book of James: "You have heard of the patience of Job" (5:11 KJV). The King James Version established the popular image of Job as a long-suffering saint. The New Testament Greek word for *"patience"* (ὑπομενή) however, means perseverance, as the NIV translates it. Along with the prophets, James uses Job as an example of those *who persevered* in the face of suffering. "As you know, we consider blessed those who have persevered. You have heard of Job's perseverance and have seen what the Lord finally brought about" (5:11 NIV). James wrote to give early Christians courage to persevere in their faith through intense persecution.

"Consider it pure joy, my brothers, whenever you face trials of many kinds, because you know that the testing of your faith develops perseverance" (1:2–3 NIV). The early Christians considered suffering for Jesus a privilege. James adds joy as a result of such testing of faith.

Job protests his lack of a response from God, and, as we saw, he shows *impatience* with the injustice of his suffering. He nevertheless perseveres. We needn't force ourselves, therefore, into a straightjacket of superficial acceptance of tragedy without murmur. When we hurt, we cry; God hears. But with Job, we can persevere, perhaps win a hearing, and experience the blessing of God's presence.

HOW TO
PREPARE FOR TRANSFORMATION

1. Reflect on your progress in recovery. How would you compare your emotional state when you began with where you are now? Identify those factors that provided you the most support. Identify those that hindered your recovery.

2. List ways in which your situation has worsened, stayed the same, and improved. Identify the reasons in each case.

3. Read Job chapters 38-41 in a modern English paraphrase, such as *The Message*. Write down key insights or thoughts as you envision the Lord speaking to you about your situation.

4. Read through the Lord's speech as part of a daily practice of meditation or personal devotion. Ask the Lord to reveal to you the lesson(s) He wants you to learn.

CHAPTER 13

TRANSFORMED

Y OUR RECOVERY HAS LED through difficult terrain, but I hope you've felt rewarded for achieving where you are now. You may still live with unanswered questions, yet, you've achieved a vantage point to help put your tragedy into perspective. A careful re-reading of the stories of people included in this book reveals not only recovery, but also transformation. Their lives have become more productive, useful, and rewarding not just despite their tragedy, but also because of it.

Because of chronic illness, Juli Grose learned to serve the Lord within her severe physical and emotional limits. Because of mental illness, Carl, driven to therapy, learned trust. Because of the unexpected death of her husband, Melissa learned to give the parts of her life she couldn't control to God. Because of her life-threatening illness, and despite her current physical limitations, Jessica's faith that God had a plan for her life enables her to appreciate life. Because of his son's accident, Pastor Nelson learned to cope with a new normal. The conclusion of Job's story also reflects that transformation.

JOB'S TRANSFORMATION

Commenting on Job 42:10-17, James writes "you have seen what the Lord finally brought about. The Lord is full of compassion and mercy" (5:11 NIV). Restored to his wife, brothers, and sisters, Job receives from the Lord double the material blessings compared to those with which he began. The Lord also restores his family, with seven sons and three beautiful daughters who are named and given an inheritance, unusual for patriarchal times. Even though He restores Job's fortunes in these visible, external ways, God also uses Job's suffering to transform him for the better, at a much deeper level.

A New Perspective

Job now knows he must give up his expectation that righteousness always results in material blessing. When his friends operated under that assumption, it caused him untold grief. His experience, confirmed by the Lord's lessons drawn from nature, has led him to a new perspective. He must learn to live in a world with evil as well as blessing, but especially without the artificial, man-made formula that righteousness inevitably produces material prosperity. We, too, must live with that awareness.

A New Attitude Toward Life

Another aspect of Job's transformed perspective is his ability to relinquish control, or what he perceived as control, over events. In chapter 1, Job sacrifices on behalf of his children, "lest they curse God in their hearts." Likely as part of his righteousness-brings-blessing theology, his thought (natural for a patriarch) focuses on his ability to ward off tragedy by acts of sacrifice on his children's behalf. Notwithstanding those sacrifices, disaster took all his possessions—and all his children. Job couldn't control events; neither can we. Learning to trust God for the future can transform our present.

A New Honesty

Throughout his discussions with his friends, Job speaks truthfully of God. Those honest words, such as those about God's injustice, deeply offend his wisdom colleagues. His desire to die because God had blocked his way (i.e., robbed his life of meaning), his determination to haul God into a court to seek justice, and his hostile images of God easily trigger in us the need to rush to God's defense. The Lord, however, has a different idea: "I am incensed at you [Eliphaz] and your two friends for you have not spoken the truth about me as did my servant Job" (42:7). So much for defending God! God condemns using theology to shut our hearts against others' suffering. He commends Job for his honesty. Learning to speak honestly, especially about God, can transform our prayers from routine requests for blessing of others into heart-felt expressions of gratitude, anguish, and love.

A New Forgiveness

His friends' lack of understanding could have led Job to bear a grudge. Instead, the Lord instructs them to "take seven bulls and seven rams and go to my servant Job and sacrifice a burnt offering for yourselves" (42:8) and to permit "my servant Job" to pray for them. We then read, "The Lord restored Job's fortunes when he prayed on behalf of his friends..." (v. 10). Job had much to learn, including how to forgive his friends. The Lord ties the restoration of double his goods, it seems, to that forgiveness. In the parable of the Unmerciful Servant (Matthew 18:23-35) Jesus teaches us to forgive others because God has forgiven us. He warns against an unforgiving spirit. Receiving God's forgiveness can transform our relationship with God to a deeper level than we've ever experienced. Our forgiving spirit will bless others.

A New Experience With God

Job's transformation culminates in a confrontation with the personal God of Abraham, Isaac, and Jacob—"the Lord." The

Lord hears our cries of suffering, as He hears Israel's cries under Egyptian bondage; He speaks to us, as He does through the prophets and in Jesus Christ; and He reveals Himself to us, as He does to Job in a tornado. Job goes back to his family and herds, but now God is real. As the Jewish philosopher Martin Buber is reported to have said, the friends gave Job religion, but Job wanted a relationship. For Christians, Jesus enables that person-to-person, intimate communion with the Living God.

Do you have a personal relationship with God? If not, why not seek the Lord to meet you at the point of your need and ask Him to reveal Himself to you? He longs for honest communication person to person. As with Job, when the Lord welcomes you into His presence, you leave transformed.

How to
Experience Transformation

1. Reflect on your perspective on life. Evaluate how strongly you assume righteousness or goodness will produce material blessing.

2. Little by little, area by area, yield your will to the Lord's sovereign control over all of your life.

3. Spend one-half to an hour in daily Bible reading and prayer, beginning with small segments of John or Mark. As you continue, develop a plan to read larger passages of Scripture. As you read, ask the Lord to teach you what He wants you to know. Record your insights in a notebook or journal.

4. Read the book of Job with an eye to seeing for yourself what it teaches. Turn to it again if tragedy strikes.

EPILOGUE

I FEEL DEEPLY GRATEFUL to the people who graciously allowed me to use their stories. To protect their privacy, except for members of my family and Dr. David Scholer, I have used fictitious names and changed some details. Because their stories show resilience, recovery, and spiritual transformation, they continue to provide hope.

Paul and Juli Grose (chapter 1) live in a specially built house to protect Juli's health as much as possible. Paul teaches piano and gives time and energy to caring for Juli. Juli's health remains fragile, however, and worsened after she contracted a common virus in 2011. She remains subject to agonizing physical pain. Her mother spends two to three hours daily in their home cleaning and keeping Juli company. Elaine, Paul's mother, and a volunteer, shop for groceries for them weekly.

"We could not have survived our twenty-eight-year-long (and counting) trial," Paul says, "without learning and applying the truth contained in God's Word. It is our daily source of sustenance and gives us perspective on what we have endured."

Mike and Andrea (chapters 2–3): The owner of Mike and Andrea's rental home decided to sell, but at an asking price above their price-range. They therefore looked for something more affordable. After Mike's mother died in April 2007, he received a small inheritance, which they used for a down payment. "God's blessing again!" according to Andrea. That August they purchased a Katrina-damaged home—all they could afford. They had to gut and clean it up again, not knowing how they would repair it, but they trusted God to provide.

And provide He did! People from their church and around the country put up sheetrock, painted, and replaced a broken fence. While the family attended their daughter's graduation, volunteers replaced the siding and put on a new roof. Plumbers offered their services; a church member gave his time to lay the donated tile. Others contributed kitchen counters and cabinets. After a long process, their house was completed in December 2010. They feel very grateful.

Mike has a lot of nearly debilitating medical conditions. God provided knee replacement in August 2008, but that left him unable to work for six months and his business never fully recovered. Yet he walked their two oldest daughters down the aisle in July 2009 and May 2011. Mike's health declined further so he started to draw Social Security Disability in November 2012.

Andrea went back to school in January 2011 to pursue a Masters' degree for teacher certification and completed her degree in December 2012. She still teaches at their church school, believing that to be her calling.

When their oldest daughter left for school in San Diego in 2004 she said, "Mom, don't let me ever forget what God has brought us through, so I can remember how much He loves me."

"Great words of advice," Andrea said. "May we never forget!"

Peter (chapter 4): From a focus on himself, after his decision to live Peter learned to serve others. "My greatest misery became my greatest ministry," he says. He attended Divorce Care and Grief Share meetings. After attending Divorce Care for a year, he agreed to serve on their board. The next two years, he served as president. He brought the "Love and Respect" marriage workshop to the group.

After six months dating a woman he met in a church singles group, they married. "We've learned to meet each other's needs," he says, "as against fighting to get our own needs met. She's been a critical part of my restoration."

"God has even conquered my childhood fear of dying," he says, "a big part of my life for decades."

Carl Johnson (chapter 6). "If it will help Christians understand mental illness," Carl said, "I'll sign." Carl referred to a legal Release of Information, allowing the author use of Carl's case file for this book. In an email to his former therapist five years after terminating therapy, Carl wrote, "Since I last saw you, I'm 1000 percent better than I was then (I was a mess!) and I have been incorporating into my life, finally, some of the things you taught." Several years after that, he reported, "I still have...(a mental disorder), but I'm dealing with it much better now."

Jessica (chapter 7): Jessica has been ill for fifteen years, a long time in her young life. She struggled with her health and prayed for a miracle to heal her. "I focused on what my life *should* look like, but I lost sight of how good my life was," she says. "Once I finally let go of my original goals, I accepted my circumstances and now trust that I can live a rich life regardless of my health.

"The last couple of years, I have learned to embrace, even love, all of me. Because of that, healing continues. I've never felt better! I still have a long list of ailments, but they do not define or limit me. That is the gift I've been given. Some days I need to rest instead of doing what I planned, but it's not negative, just my reality. I love life and am grateful for so *many* gifts I've received. Life is a journey, and I know I will continue to blossom into the beautiful woman God intended me to be."

The Rev. John Nelson (chapter 7) reports: "After three years of recovery, Ron did well in college courses. He worked for a home medical equipment provider. Because he used a chair himself, customers related to him better than to able-bodied sales people. Local TV programs featured him as an example of a person who overcame great odds. When the company sold out, and he was let go, he grieved a year.

"During the past several years, Ron's health has declined. Unable to work, he continues to live alone in his own home. He depends on caregivers to get him up, put him to bed, and do basic housekeeping chores. He has a few dependable, able-bodied friends who drop by to see him and they all play poker one night a month.

"Ron's medical needs dramatically increased this year. A large infection developed that threatened to enter the bone, travel to the brain, and prove fatal. Surgery removed it, but Ron's extended recovery time lying in bed created pneumonia—his lung collapsed and filled with fluid.

"Because of Ron's quadriplegia, he could not cough fluid out of his lungs. Even as early as twenty-eight years ago, his mom and I regularly performed a 'quad cough' on him, synchronizing his cough with a type of Heimlich maneuver from the front. Ron has since learned to do this maneuver himself but the procedure creates other issues; a vicious cycle ensues which puts him back in bed where his collapsed lung again fills with fluid.

"Intense physical care routines for Ron produce daily frustration among family members, especially his mother. Quad cough treatments take time, especially through the night, and drain energy. She also tries to maintain a normal daytime routine at her home. She must provide service essential to Ron, but without becoming an enabler.

"When Ron is healthy, he has creative ideas and valuable insights, but his survival is tenuous. His oxygen saturation levels regularly drop into lethal readings; mentally, he suffers from depression much of the time. Even at this, Ron's night caregiver, his mother, believes the countless prayers offered to God on their behalf provide extraordinary strength for them to carry on.

The family of **Dr. David M. Scholer (chapter 7)**, the Fuller Theological Seminary community, and the congregation of First Baptist Church, Pasadena, CA held a memorial service for the much beloved professor of New Testament on August 30, 2008. "David Scholer was a distinguished scholar, teacher, administrator, and mentor," says Richard J. Muow, president of Fuller. "His passion for New Testament Scholarship was contagious, and he modeled in his life the joy of the truths he taught, even through suffering."

"I have an incurable disease," he would tell his students on the first day of class—and then he would teach New Testament in a rasping voice with such joy and conviction the many students were deeply moved by his example.

"In the years since my husband's passing," says **Melissa (chapter 8)**, "I struggled with feeling monotone, incapable of intense joy or sadness. Although never in a self-destruct mode, I couldn't find joy in the everyday moments of life. If I was to be a witness of God's grace, I knew I must look life in the eye again. God expects me to do well. Daily internal battles mean daily prayer and handing it to Him. The only way I fail is if I quit. And, by the grace of God, every day gets better."

Hank (chapter 9) writes: "After Laurie died, I focused on recovering my balance. I established my life as a single for a year. I expected to gradually recover 'living well,' so I paid attention to whether things were going the way I expected. I also wrote a good deal about my experience to help me compare reality with my expectations.

"When I began dating again, a year later, it held no charms for me. I had not been good at it as a teenager and my skills had not improved over fifty years of not practicing. But when Fran walked into Starbucks, where we agreed to meet, January 2005, my dating problems ended. We married December 2005. The best way to enter a new relationship is to close the previous relationship with affection and honor. I had loved Laurie well and, in one short year, had grieved her death as fully as I could. Episodes of grief continue, of course; Fran honors that. I seem to have been able, in the ten years since Laurie's death, to lay down the old good marriage and to build a good new marriage. Fran and I are colleagues in building that marriage as well as lovers in enjoying it.

"As an unexpected advantage of my experience of grief," Hank says, "I understand the grief of others my age. They share things with me they would not share with others. I never sought that personal understanding, but since it found me, I offer it to others as a gift."

Beverly (chapter 10) has since died, but her son writes: "I knew my mother saw a psychiatrist. I understood, however, that it was for treatment of a chemical imbalance. I believe my mother was able to function effectively because of her faith as well as the counsel she received from her pastor and the medical community."

After **Mary (chapter 12)** completed a Master's degree, she began a counseling practice. She also counsels for a non-profit, as well as managing specific programs for them.

Mary's parents moved closer to her after their health deteriorated so she visits them daily. Although Mary wants them to remain independent as long as they desire it, she found worrying about their wellbeing stressful. To cope, she joined an active community service organization. Because she serves with people who know nothing about her personal life she can freely serve the homeless at the local shelter, serve Thanksgiving dinner to the children of an inner city elementary school and their families or help plan an event to honor veterans. That provides a feel-good escape for her.

Mary's third husband, a clinical psychologist, supported her through a period of fighting a life-threatening disease.

ACKNOWLEDGEMENTS

I FEEL DEEPLY GRATEFUL to the late Professor Nahum N. Glatzer of Brandeis University, whose course on Job when I was a graduate student many decades ago first aroused my passion for the book of Job.

Except for the gracious permission of those I interviewed, and others, my book would lack the rich examples of how people today experience tragedy and its transformation. I appreciate their trust in me to tell their stories.

I am also deeply grateful to my early writing mentor, Cecil Murphey, from whom I had the most to learn. In addition to publishing well over 130 books, many of them bestsellers, Cecil devotes his time and talent to mentor new writers, a ministry from which I benefitted.

I am also grateful for the early editorial work of Patrick Borders (http://www.platinumprose.com), who helped me discipline my writing, as well as for the later editorial work of Jill Kelly, PhD, (http://www.jillkelly.com; aracnet.com), who helped me shape this book into its present form. Rodger K. Bufford, PhD, George Fox University, provided invaluable insights through his consultations over my content, especially during the early stages of writing.

My critique group members Billie Reynolds, Shirley Dechaine, and Paul Hailey, provided helpful suggestions, improvements, and corrections to my manuscript. My volunteer advisors, Spike Bailey, Daniel Sweeney, PhD, Joan Schultz, LPC, and the Rev. Norman Lawson provided expert guidance and encouragement.

I acknowledge my gratitude to the Rev. John Fischer, now deceased, who encouraged me to write a book on Job, and to Leslie Stobbe, Literary Agent, for his advice in helping me write this book.

Finally, I thank my wife Elaine for her support, encouragement, and occasional, but critical, intervention to help me make sense of my thoughts.

ENDNOTES

CHAPTER 1

1. "Chronic fatigue syndrome, or CFS, is a debilitating and complex disorder characterized by profound fatigue that is not improved by bed rest and that may be worsened by physical or mental activity. Symptoms affect several body systems and may include weakness, muscle pain, impaired memory and/or mental concentration, and insomnia, which can result in reduced participation in daily activities." http://www.cdc.gov/cfs/ Pastor Jim Andrews tells more of their story in *Polishing God's Monuments: Pillars of Hope for Punishing Times*, (Wapwallopen, PA: Shepherd Press, 2007), now available at www.jim-andrews.org.

CHAPTER 3

1. *The Oregonian*, September 2, 2005, 1.

2. http://www.hintv.com/article/2011/12/26/2011-unusual-year-weather?htp=hp_t2 Accessed 2/11/2012.

3. *The Book of Job: A New Translation According to the Traditional Hebrew Text with Introductions*. Moshe Greenberg, Jonas C. Greenfield, and Nahum M. Sarna (Philadelphia: The Jewish Publication Society, 1980). Because of its close adherence to the Hebrew, unless otherwise indicated, I use this text throughout.

4. Norman Habel, *The Book of Job: A Commentary*, The Old Testament Library (Philadelphia: Westminster, 1985), 87.

5. Habel, *Job*, 88

6. Habel, *Job*, 92.

7. David J. A. Clines, *Job 1-20*, Word Biblical Commentary (Dallas: Word Books, 1989), 33.

8. *The New York Times*, "Survivors of Katrina Turning to Suicide" http://www.nytimes.com/2005/12/27/world/americas/27ihtkatrina.html?r=1&pagewanted=print. Archived.

CHAPTER 4

1. To stress his role as prosecutor, the Book of Job always refers to "The" Satan, but to avoid confusion, I will use the simple term *Satan*.

2. "The key term Job selects to characterize his lot is *'amal*, 'misery/ trouble'... The *'amal* of Job's affliction reaches such a level of intensity that Job considers it grounds for incantations calling on sinister forces to revoke his origins." Habel, *Job*, 109-110.

3. Johannes Pedersen, *Israel: Its Life and Culture I-II*, (London, UK: Oxford University Press: Geoffrey Cumberlege, 1926), 167.

4. 3:11, 12, 16, 20. The Hebrew of v. 23 omits "Why does He give life..." , but it is understood.

5. Artur Weiser, *The Psalms: A Commentary*, The Old Testament Library, trans. Herman Hartwell (Philadelphia: Westminster, 1962), 82.

6. *Grief and Pain in the Plan of God: Christian Assurance and the Message of Lamentations*. Walter C. Kaiser, Jr. (Ross-shire, UK: Christian Focus Publications, 2004), 38-39. See also his "Eight Kinds of Suffering in the Old Testament," in *Suffering and the Goodness of God*, Christopher W. Morgan and Robert A. Peterson, Eds., (Wheaton, IL: Crossway Books, 2008), 65-78, and, in the same volume, his "Suffering and the Goodness of God in the Old Testament," 47-63.

7. *Severe* refers to a person diagnosed with the number of symptoms substantially higher than the minimum required (5) to make the diagnosis, with the intensity of symptoms causing serious distress and proving unmanageable, and which markedly interfere with social and occupational functioning. American Psychiatric Association, *Diagnostic and Statistical Manual of Mental Disorders*, 5th ed., (Washington, DC: American Psychiatric Association, 2013), 188. See also 160-161.

CHAPTER 5

1. "The Relationship of Adverse Childhood Experiences to Adult Medical Disease, Psychiatric Disorders, and Sexual Behavior: Implications for Healthcare," Vincent J. Felitti and Robert F. Anda, in *The Impact of Early Life Trauma on Health and Disease: The Hidden Epidemic*, Ruth Lanius, Eric Vermetten, and Clare Pain, Eds., (Cambridge, UK: Cambridge University Press, 2010), 77-87. Kindle e-book.

2. http://www.karenkoehlerblog.com/2011/09/why-do-people-sue-part-2-david-balls-response/

3. Text note on Job 7:6, *The Book of Job*, (Philadelphia, PA: Jewish Publication Society, 1980), 11.

4. Joni Eareckson Tada, *The God I Love: A Lifetime of Walking with Jesus* (Grand Rapids, MI: Zondervan, 2003), 167-169.

5. Habel, *Job*, 131. Clines, *Job 1-20,* 138-9. Clines calls attention to Proverbs 14:30: "A heart at peace gives life to the body, but envy (the same word as Eliphaz's 'passion' in 5:2) rots the bones."

6. Habel, *Job*, 131.

7. The passage G. F. Handel famously applied to Christ in his *Messiah* aria, "I Know That My Redeemer Liveth."

8. Habel lists twelve legal expressions in Job's speech of Chapters 9 and 10, *Job*, 188f.

9. R. E. Butman, "Anger," in *Baker Encyclopedia of Psychology and Counseling*, 2nd ed., D. G. Benner and P. C. Hill, Eds. (Grand Rapids: Baker, 1985, 1999), 81.

10. R. E. Butman, "Anger," in *Baker Encyclopedia of Psychology*, ed. D. G. Benner (Grand Rapids: Baker, 1985), 58. Statement omitted in later addition.

11. See Joseph Le Doux, *The Emotional Brain: The Mysterious Underpinnings of Emotional Life,* (New York: Simon and Schuster, 1966), 164, 166. I have drawn on information shared by Brad Barris, Ph.D., "Understanding Anger: Managing Aggression and Hostility," CorTexT/MindMatters Educational Seminar, September 26, 2000.

12. B. M. Hartung, "Working Through," in *Dictionary of Pastoral Care and Counseling*, ed. Rodney J. Hunter (Nashville: Abingdon Press, 1990), 1338.

13. Joni Eareckson Tada, "A Grace Disguised," Ockenga Institute, Gordon-Conwell Theological Seminary, Hamilton, MA, June 27, 2003. Used with permission.

14. D. G. Bagby, "Anger," in *Dictionary of Pastoral Care and Counseling*, ed. Rodney J. Hunter (Nashville: Abingdon Press, 1990), 41.

15. B. M. Hartung, "Working Through," in *Dictionary of Pastoral Care and Counseling*, ed. Rodney J. Hunter (Nashville: Abingdon Press, 1990), 1338.

CHAPTER 6

1. I am indebted to Habel, *The Book of Job,* for his characterizations of Job's experience of God.

2. Habel, *Job*, 132, 145. Clines, *Job 1-20*, 142.

3. Habel, *Job*, 272.

Chapter 7

1. Even advice from medical and counseling professionals fell short. When Jessica's headache persisted twenty-four hours a day through that time, a prominent Midwestern clinic she visited diagnosed her ailment as "sudden onset chronic daily headaches with migrainous components." She was unimpressed with their diagnosis. A doctor there also told her this was something she would have to live with the rest of her life, advice she refused to accept. A therapist Jessica and her mother saw jointly asked if Jessica were making her symptoms up, perhaps to gain attention. Active in school sports before the infection, Jessica needed no medical crisis to gain attention.

2. By juxtaposing incongruous elements of revelation (a word, a sound, deep sleep, a terror, a wind, an apparition, a voice), the author of Job makes Eliphaz's well-intentioned efforts a parody of those who rely on private personal revelation as their authority in spiritual matters. See Habel, *Job*, 121-123.

3. Eliphaz's self-regard as an authority shows in his use of language. The first-person pronoun "I," ordinarily part of the verb in Hebrew: "I would appeal," can be used separately for emphasis. Eliphaz uses that separated first-person pronoun here: "But if it were I, *I* . . . " "The first-person pronoun is heavily stressed, being repeated in different ways four times. This is typical of Eliphaz's style." John E. Hartley, *The Book of Job*, New International Commentary on the Old Testament (Grand Rapids, MI: Eerdmans, 1988), 120, n. 8.

4. "There is an ironic twist in Job's interpretation which translates Eliphaz' traditional but sympathetic analysis of Job's plight into evidence of insensitivity and deception." Habel, *Job*, 141. Job reinterprets in a negative light the words *anguish* (6:2. Cf. 5:2), *hope* (6:6. Cf. 4:6), *success* (6:13. Cf. 5:12), *crush* (6:9. Cf. 4:19), and *fear* (6:14. Cf. 4:6). A depressed person likely will interpret any positive efforts at comfort in a negative way.

5. Sermon: David M. Scholer, "Living with Cancer," First Baptist Church, 75 N Marengo St., Pasadena, CA, September 18, 2005, CD-ROM.

6. Habel, *Job*, 204. The Jewish Publication Society Edition (1980) of *The Book of Job* notes on 11:6, "Meaning of the Heb. Uncertain."

7. See Habel, *Job*, 208.

8. Jack Kahn, *Job's Illness: Loss, Grief and Integration: A Psychological Interpretation* (Oxford, UK: Pergamon Press), 1975, 64. I am indebted to Kahn for the idea of Job's process of recovery.

CHAPTER 8

1. Habel, *Job*, 399.
2. Habel, *Job*, 393
3. Habel, Job, 393.
4. Leader of the German Ostrogoths and raised with Roman education and culture, Theodoric also followed the teachings of the British monk Arius (circa 260-336 AD), who taught that "only the Father is God, strictly speaking; the Son, along with everything that exists, is created into being through the will of the Father..." "Aryanism," in *Encyclopedia of Christian Theology*, vol. I, ed. Jean-Yves Lacoste (New York: Routledge, 2005), 91. Orthodox Christians who believe Jesus is the eternal, incarnate, uncreated Son still consider Arius's teaching heresy. Earlier, Boethius had opposed the violent Goths and written a treatise *On the Catholic Faith* to counter Arianism.
5. V. E. Watts, trans., *The Consolation of Philosophy* by Anicius Manlius Severinus Boethius, (Harmondsworth: Penguin, 1976), 7-18. I have used Watts' translation. See also P. G. Walsh, *Boethius: The Consolation of Philosophy*, (Oxford, UK: Oxford University Press, 1999), xi-xx. Walsh points to Boethius's zeal for dealing with corruption, his repeated censure of Theodoric, and his imperious attitude as contributing to his downfall and to his being charged with treason.
6. Philosophy Consoling Boethius and Fortune Turning the Wheel, by Coëtivy Master (Henri de Vulcop?) (French, active about 1450 - 1485) Google Cultural Institute Art Project, http://www.googleartproject.com/artist/coetivy-master/6913132/. Current location: The J. Paul Getty Museum, Los Angeles. In the public domain, available from Wikimedia Commons, http://www.wickimediacommons.org In the depiction of The Wheel of Life at the Cathedral, Cologne, Germany, an aged man on the right pushes upward against the spoke to slow the wheel's progress, as a young man pushes up against the spoke on the left in order to hurry his ascent, and the man on top has wealth enough to give alms to the poor.
7. "Let Fortune turn her wheel as pleases her." Dante Alighieri. *The Divine Comedy of Dante Alighieri*, Great Books of the Western World, vol. 21, trans. Charles Eliot Norton, (Chicago: Encyclopedia Britannica, 1952), 22, canto xv, 95. Dante Alighieri lived from 1265 to 1321. The Wheel of Life gave perspective to people extending into the time of Shakespeare (1564-1616). "Life was imagined—and often depicted in woodcuts and engravings—as a great wheel," says Marjorie Gerber, Harvard professor of English and American literature. "Each man and each woman's life reached a point of greatest height, greatest prosperity, from which he or she would ultimately fall. We hear a great deal about this kind of tragedy in *King Lear*." Marjorie Gerber, *Shakespeare after All* (New York: Pantheon Books, 2004), 661.

Chapter 9

1. Habel, *Job*, 404.
2. Habel, *Job*, 409.
3. See Exodus 17:6; Deuteronomy 32:13.
4. Habel, *Job*, 410.
5. Habel, *Job*, 412.
6. "In the army there is much less room for debate and compromise; in the army, the king gives orders and his troops obey." Clines, *Job 21-37*, 995.
7. Art. "Shame," R. L. Timpe, in *Baker Encyclopedia of Psychology & Counseling*, eds. D. G. Benner and P. C. Hill, 2nd ed., (Grand Rapids: Baker Book House, 1999), 1114.
8. Email communication.
9. T. L. Martin and K. J. Doka, *Men Don't Cry... Women Do: Transcending Gender Stereotypes of Grief*, (Philadelphia: Bruner/Mazel, 2000), 36.
10. Martin and Doka, *Men Don't Cry*, 40. The authors give an example on page 11.

Chapter 10

1. Many scholars see the Elihu chapters (32-27) as a later addition. For those arguments and rebuttal, see D. J. A. Clines, *Job 21-37*, Word Biblical Commentary (Nashville, TN: Thomas Nelson, 2006), 708f. Habel interprets Elihu as a hotheaded fool, contrary to how he sees himself. *Job*, 443-447. For another view, see Clines, 709f. Newsom sees these chapters as a response to the book written by a later reader. *The Book of Job: A Contest of Moral Imaginations* (New York: Oxford University Press, 2003), 200-233.
2. Habel, *Job*, 459.
3. Habel, *Job*, 466.
4. "Thus the materials in the legal framework of this speech represented a formal legal response designed to convince Job of Elihu's authority, compassion, and expertise in the case. Beneath this forensic façade of good will, however, the arrogance of Elihu was subtly exposed by the author." Habel, *Job*, 460-461.
5. Nicky Cruz with Jamie Buckingham, *Run, Baby, Run* (Orlando, FL: Bridge-Logos, 1968), 117.
6. Cruz, *Run, Baby, Run*, 122.
7. Cruz, *Run, Baby, Run*, 123.

CHAPTER 11

1. Habel, *Job*, 530-532. "As a defense, the speech also makes repeated allusions, innuendos, and ironic hints at earlier claims and accusations of Job." 530.

2. "...Job (and the reader!) is put in his place—not by a rebuke, not by a warning against questioning God, but by the gracious advent of God who allows himself to be seen inasmuch as that is humanly possible." Gerald H. Wilson, *Job*, New International Biblical Commentary (Peabody, MA: Hendrickson, 2007), 423.

3. "My Pilgrimage from Atheism to Theism: A Discussion between Anthony Flew and Gary Habermas," *Philosophia Christi, Journal of the Evangelical Philosophical Society* (Winter 2004), 6 (2), 197-212. www.philchristi.org/library/articles.asp?pid=33.

4. Clines, *Job 21-37*, 850, note on 23e. Habel translates, "He does not answer," *Job*, 516. Both translations require emending, i.e., changing, the Hebrew text. The Jewish Publication Society translation (1980) I use throughout translates as "He does not torment."

5. Habel, *Job,* 536.

6. Habel, *Job,* 534. "In a world where paradox and incongruity are integral to its design, there is no simplistic answer to the problem of innocent suffering."

7. "[The wild ass] stands for everything opposed to the world of human order and culture." Newsom, quoted by Clines, *Job 38-42*, 1121. Clines stresses the varieties of life in the Lord's creation in the Lord's speech.

8. Habel, *Job*, 534. "Job's complaint that the innocent suffer unjustly is never refuted. It stands side by side with the answers of Yahweh as part of the paradox of that design." Habel, *Job*, 535.

9. The Jewish Publication Society (1980) note to translation of 41:4 (41:12 Eng.): "Meaning of the Heb. uncertain." English translators have changed the numbering of verses in this passage. Although I give the English references, I continue to use the 1980 Jewish Publication Society translation.

CHAPTER 12

1. Habel, *Job*, 581. "Perhaps the author employed this expression to remind the audience of the original scheme devised by Yahweh and the Satan to test Job's integrity and that Job is in fact suspicious of some such plan."

2. Habel, *Job,* 582.

BIBLIOGRAPHY

Alighieri, Dante. *The Divine Comedy of Dante Alighieri.* Translated by Charles E. Norton. *Great Books of the Western World*, edited by Robert M. Hutchings, vol. 21. Chicago: Encyclopedia Britannica, 1952.

American Psychiatric Association. *Diagnostic and Statistical Manual of Mental Disorders*, 5th ed. Washington, DC: American Psychiatric Association, 2013.

"Aryanism," in Jean-Yves Lacoste, Ed., *Encyclopedia of Christian Theology*, vol. I. New York: Routledge, 2005, 90-92.

Bagby, D. G. "Anger," in Rodney J. Hunter, Ed. *Dictionary of Pastoral Care and Counseling.* Nashville, TN: Abingdon Press, 1990.

Barris, Brad. "Understanding Anger: Managing Aggression and Hostility," CorTexT/MindMatters Educational Seminar, Portland, OR, September 26, 2000.

Brehony, Kathleen. *After the Darkest Hour: How Suffering Begins the Journey to Wisdom.* New York: Henry Holt and Company, 2000.

Butman, R. E. "Anger," in D. G. Benner and P. C. Hill, Eds., *Baker Encyclopedia of Psychology and Counseling*, 2nd Edition. Grand Rapids, MI: Baker, 1985, 1999.

Centers for Disease Control and Prevention. "Chronic Fatigue Syndrome." See http://www.cdc.gov/cfs/general/index.html

Clines, D. J. A. *Job 1-20. Word Biblical Commentary.* Dallas, TX: Word Books, 1989.

Clines, D. J. A. *Job 21-37. Word Biblical Commentary.* Nashville, TN: Thomas Nelson, 2006.

Clines, D. J. A. *Job 38-42. Word Biblical Commentary.* Nashville, TN: Thomas Nelson, 2011.

Coëtivy Master (Henri de Vulcop?) (French, active about 1450 - 1485). Philosophy Consoling Boethius and Fortune Turning the Wheel. Google Cultural Art Institute Project, http://www.googleartproject. com/artist/coetivy-master/6913132/. Current location: The J. Paul Getty Museum, Los Angeles. In the public domain. Available from Wikimedia Commons, http://www.wickimediacommons.org.

Cruz, Nicky, with Jamie Buckingham. *Run, Baby, Run*. Orlando, FL: Bridge-Logos, 1968.

Douglas, Jack, Jr., Scott Dodd, and Martin Merzer. "City Spirals into Chaos." *The Oregonian*, September 2, 2005, 1.

Felitti, Vincent J., and Robert F. Anda. "The Relationship of Adverse Childhood Experiences to Adult Medical Disease, Psychiatric Disorders, and Sexual Behavior: Implications for Healthcare," in Lanius, Ruth, Eric Vermetten, and Clare Pain, Eds. *The Hidden Epidemic: The Impact of Early Life Trauma on Health and Disease*. Cambridge, UK: Cambridge University Press, 2010.

Flew, Anthony. "My Pilgrimage from Atheism to Theism: A Discussion between Anthony Flew and Gary Habermas," in *Philosophia Christi, Journal of the Evangelical Philosophical Society* (vol. 6 no. 2, Winter 2004), 197-212. Retrieved from www.philchristi.org/library/articles. asp?pid=33.

Gerber, Marjorie. *Shakespeare after All*. New York: Pantheon Books, 2004.

Greenberg, Moshe, Jonas C. Greenfield, and Nahum M. Sarna. *The Book of Job: A New Translation According to the Traditional Hebrew Text with Introductions*. Philadelphia: The Jewish Publication Society, 1980.

Habel, Norman C. *The Book of Job: A Commentary. The Old Testament Library*. Philadelphia: Westminster, 1985.

Hartley, John E. *The Book of Job, New International Commentary on the Old Testament*. Grand Rapids, MI: Eerdmans, 1988.

Hartung, B. M. "Working Through," in Rodney J. Hunter, Ed., *Dictionary of Pastoral Care and Counseling*. Nashville, TN: Abingdon Press, 1990.

HINTV. http://www.hintv.com/article/2011/12/26/2011-unusual-year-weather?htp=hp_t2 Retrieved 2/11/12.

Jung, Carl G. *Answer to Job*. Translated by R. F. C. Hull. *Bollingen Series*. Princeton, NJ: Princeton University Press, ninth printing, 1991.

Kahn, Jack H. *Job's Illness: Loss, Grief, and Integration: A Psychological Interpretation*. Oxford, UK: Pergamon Press, 1975.

Kaiser, Walter C., Jr. *Grief and Pain in the Plan of God: Christian Assurance and the Message of Lamentations*. Ross-shire, UK: Christian Focus Publications, 2004. First published by Moody Press, Chicago, IL, 1982.

Koehler, Karen. See http://www.karenkoehlerblog.com/2011/09/why-do-people-sue-part-2-david-balls-response/

Le Doux, Joseph. *The Emotional Brain: The Mysterious Underpinnings of Emotional Life*. New York: Simon and Schuster, 1966.

Martin, T. L., and J. Doka. *Men Don't Cry... Women Do: Transcending Gender Stereotypes of Grief*. Philadelphia: Bruner/Mazel, 2000.

Newsom, Carol A. *The Book of Job: A Contest of Moral Imaginations*. Oxford, UK: Oxford University Press, 2003.

Pedersen, Johannes. *Israel: Its Life and Culture I-II*. London, UK: Oxford University Press: Geoffrey Cumberlege, 1926.

Scholer, David M. "Living with Cancer." Sermon, First Baptist Church, 75 N Marengo Ave., Pasadena, CA, September 18, 2005.

Tada, Joni Eareckson. "A Grace Disguised." Lecture, Ockenga Institute, Gordon-Conwell Theological Seminary, Hamilton, MA, June 27, 2003.

Tada, Joni Eareckson. *The God I Love: A Lifetime of Walking with Jesus*. Grand Rapids, MI: Zondervan, 2003.

The New York Times, "Survivors of Katrina Turning to Suicide." http://www.nytimes.com/2005/12/27/world/americas/27ihtkatrina.html?r=1&pagewanted=print, 1. Archived.

Timpe, R. L. "Shame," in D. G. Benner, and P. C. Hill, Eds., *Baker Encyclopedia of Psychology & Counseling*, 2nd ed. Grand Rapids: Baker Book House, 1999.

Walsh, P. G. *Boethius: The Consolation of Philosophy*. *Oxford World Classics*. Oxford, UK: Oxford University Press, 1999.

Watts, V. E. *The Consolation of Philosophy by Anicius Manlius Severinus Boethius*. Harmondsworth, Middlesex UK: Penguin, 1976.

Weiser, Artur. *The Psalms: A Commentary. The Old Testament Library.* Translated by Herman Hartwell. Philadelphia: Westminster, 1962.

Wilson, Gerald H. *Job. New International Biblical Commentary.* First published jointly by Hendrickson Publishers, Peabody, MA and Paternoster Press, Milton Keyes, UK, 2007.

INDEX

HOW TO CONTACT GORDON:

For speaking, workshops, and teaching, readers may contact the author at Facebook: https://www.facebook.com/gordon.grose

Linkedin: www.linkedin.com/pub/gordon-grose/1b/340/130

Google Plus: https://plus.google.com/+GordonGrose/about

Additional copies of Tragedy Transformed may be purchased at www.tragedytransformed.com, and at
Amazon at www.amazon.com
Barnes and Noble: www.bn.com
Christian Book Distributors: www.christianbook.com
Powell's Books www.powells.com

Pastors, Bible study and small group leaders: to obtain a free download of questions for discussion based on this book, go to www.tragedytransformed.com.
Tragedy Transformed: Questions for Discussion by Gordon S. Grose

See also www.gordongrose.com for Gordon's blogs on Job, death and dying, mental illness, and recovery from addiction.

Each book purchased at full retail price contributes $1.00 to care for orphans in Africa